REAL WORLD HEALTH CARE

AN ECONOMICS READER FROM *DOLLARS & SENSE*

EDITED BY DANIEL FIRESIDE, CHRIS STURR,
AND THE *DOLLARS & SENSE* COLLECTIVE

REAL WORLD HEALTH CARE

Copyright 2008 by Economic Affairs Bureau, Inc.
All rights reserved. No portions of this book may be reproduced without prior permission from Economic Affairs Bureau.

Published by:
Economic Affairs Bureau, Inc.
Dollars & Sense
29 Winter Street
Boston, MA 02108
617-447-2177
dollars@dollarsandsense.org
www.dollarsandsense.org

Real World Health Care is edited by the Dollars & Sense Collective, which also publishes *Dollars & Sense* magazine and the classroom books *Real World Macro, Real World Micro, Real World Globalization, Real World Banking, Real World Latin America, The Wealth Inequality Reader, The Environment in Crisis, Introduction to Political Economy, Unlevel Playing Fields: Understanding Wage Inequality and Discrimination, Striking a Balance: Work, Family, Life,* and *Grassroots Journalism*.

The 2008 Collective:
Arpita Banerjee, Amee Chew, Ben Collins, Ben Greenberg, Daniel Fireside, Amy Gluckman, Mary Jirmanus, James McBride, James Miehls, John Miller, Larry Peterson, Linda Pinkow, Paul Piwko, Smriti Rao, Alejandro Reuss, Dave Ryan, Bryan Snyder, Chris Sturr, Ramaa Vasudevan, and Jeanne Winner.

Cover design: Chris Sturr
Production: Chris Sturr
Editorial asssistance: Carrie Battan, Heather Boersma, and Jason Son

Manufactured by Lightning Source
Printed in U.S.A.

CONTENTS

1. Paying More, Getting Less   *Joel Harrison*   1

2. Don't Blame the Minimum Wage   *Paddy Quick*   6

3. Inequality: Bad for Your Health   *Ichiro Kawachi*   8

4. What is "Comparative Advantage"?   *Ramaa Vasudevan*   16

5. The Care Gap   *Robert Drago*   18

6. The 800-Pound McDonald in the Room   *Helen Scharber*   25

7. The Opposite of Insurance   *James Woolman*   27

8. Medicare and Medicaid Cuts   *Sam Uretsky*   30

9. Katrina Hits Cancer Alley   *Monique Harden/Ben Greenberg*   33

10. Medicare D Gets an "F"   *James Woolman/James McBride*   40

11. What's Good for Wal-Mart   *John Miller*   43

12. Health Care Security in NYC   *Hannah Clark*   48

13. Ill and Insolvent   *Kayty Himmelstein*   50

14. Wal-Mart Welfare   *Jenna Wright*   51

15. ABCs of AIDS Prevention   *Jessica Weisberg*   54

16. African Americans and Social Security   *William E. Spriggs*   58

17. Job-Based Health Insurance   *James Woolman*   63

18. Victories for Home Health Care Workers   *Stu Schneider*   66

19. Pricing the Priceless   *Lisa Heinzerling/Frank Ackerman*   70

20. Drug Prices in Crisis   *Dean Baker*   75

21. Cause of Death: Inequality   *Alejandro Reuss*   81

22. The Social Relations of Health and Disease   *Jeanne Winner*   85

23. "Raise the Alarm Loudly"   *Akin Jimoh*   89

24. Out of the Ashes   *Ochoro E. Otunnu/Sunday Dare/Akin Jimoh*   93

25. Sustainable Sanitation   *Laura Orlando*   97

26. Putting Names on the Numbers   *Lisa Climan/Adria Scharf*   102

27. Making Patients Pay   *Ellen Frank*   104

28. Spending #1, Performance #37   *Phineas Baxandall*   110

29. Medical Residents Organize   *Stephanie Greenwood*   113

30. Social Movements: Good for Your Health   *Thad Williamson*   114

31. Price Gouging: It's Just Supply and Demand   *Marc Breslow*   116

32. The Growth Consensus Unravels   *Jonathan Rowe*   118

33. The "Natural Rate" of Unemployment   *Robert Pollin*   124

Article 1

PAYING MORE, GETTING LESS
How much is the sick U.S. health care system costing you?

JOEL A. HARRISON
May/June 2008*

By any measure, the United States spends an enormous amount of money on health care. Here are a few of those measures. Last year, U.S. health care spending exceeded 16% of the nation's GDP. To put U.S. spending into perspective: the United States spent 15.3% of GDP on health care in 2004, while Canada spent 9.9%, France 10.7%, Germany 10.9%, Sweden 9.1%, and the United Kingdom 8.7%. Or consider per capita spending: the United States spent $6,037 per person in 2004, compared to Canada at $3,161, France at $3,191, Germany at $3,169, and the U.K. at $2,560.

By now the high overall cost of health care in the United States is broadly recognized. And many Americans are acutely aware of how much they pay for their own care. Those without health insurance face sky-high doctor and hospital bills and ever more aggressive collection tactics—when they receive care at all. Those who are fortunate enough to have insurance experience steep annual premium hikes along with rising deductibles and co-pays, and, all too often, a well-founded fear of losing their coverage should they lose a job or have a serious illness in the family.

Still, Americans may well underestimate the degree to which they subsidize the current U.S. health care system out of their own pockets. And almost no one recognizes that even people without health insurance pay substantial sums into the system today. If more people understood the full size of the health care bill that they as individuals are already paying—and for a system that provides seriously inadequate care to millions of Americans—then the corporate opponents of a universal single-payer system might find it far more difficult to frighten the public about the costs of that system. In other words, to recognize the advantages of a single-payer system, we have to understand how the United States funds health care and health research and how much it actually costs us today.

Paying Through the Taxman

The U.S. health care system is typically characterized as a largely private-sector system, so it may come as a surprise that more than 60% of the $2 trillion annual U.S. health care bill is paid through taxes, according to a 2002 analysis published in Health Affairs by Harvard Medical School associate professors Steffie Woolhandler and David Himmelstein. Tax dollars pay for Medicare and Medicaid, for the Veterans Administration and the Indian Health Service. Tax dollars pay for health cov-

---

* Dates refer to when the article appeared in *Dollars & Sense* magazine. Author biographies are current as of the time the article appeared in the magazine.

erage for federal, state, and municipal government employees and their families, as well as for many employees of private companies working on government contracts. Less visible but no less important, the tax deduction for employer-paid health insurance, along with other health care-related tax deductions, also represents a form of government spending on health care. It makes little difference whether the government gives taxpayers (or their employers) a deduction for their health care spending, on the one hand, or collects their taxes then pays for their health care, either directly or via a voucher, on the other. Moreover, tax dollars also pay for critical elements of the health care system apart from direct care—Medicare funds much of the expensive equipment hospitals use, for instance, along with all medical residencies.

All told, then, tax dollars already pay for at least $1.2 trillion in annual U.S. health care expenses. Since federal, state, and local governments collect about $3.48

What Americans Pay into the U.S. Health Care System Today		Household Income Level		
		$25,000	$50,000	$75,000
Share and Amount of Income Going to Health Care via Taxes Alone		9.0% ($2,425)	9.8% ($5,300)	10.7% ($8,633)
Share and Amount of Total Wage Packet Going to Health Care for Households with Insurance	Individual	22.0% ($6,904)	16.8% ($9,779)	15.4% ($13,112)
	Family	37.2% ($14,531)	26.4% ($17,406)	22.3% ($20,749)

Note: The share of total wage packet going to health care was calculated as follows:
$$\frac{\text{(amount of total tax burden going to health + annual health insurance premium)}}{\text{(annual salary + payroll tax [FICA and Medicare] + annual health insurance premium)}}$$
Further details of the calculations are available at www.dollarsandsense.org.

trillion annually in taxes of all kinds—income, sales, property, corporate—that means that more than one third (34.4%) of the aggregate tax revenues collected in the United States go to pay for health care.

Beyond their direct payments to health care providers and health insurance companies, then, Americans already make a sizeable annual payment into the health care system via taxes. How much does a typical household contribute to the country's health care system altogether? Of course, households pay varying amounts in taxes depending on income and many other factors. Moreover, some households have no health insurance coverage; others do have coverage for which they may pay some or all of the premium cost. What I aim to do here is to estimate the average size of the health care cost burden for households at different income levels, both those with job-based health cov-erage and those with no coverage.

Note that the estimates in the table (above) do not include out-of-pocket expenses. For those with health insurance, these include co-pays, deductibles, and uncovered expenses (consider, for example, that even my high-end policy does not cover commonly used home medical equipment such as oxygen). For those without insurance, of course, out-of-pocket expenses include their full hospital, doctor, and pharmacy bills.

The first row ("Share and Amount of Income Going to Health Care via Taxes Alone") shows how much of the total tax burden on households at three income levels goes into the nation's health care system. In other words, a family with an annual income of $50,000 that has no health insurance nonetheless contributes nearly 10% of its income to health care merely by paying typical income, payroll, sales, excise, and other taxes. A person who earns about $25,000 a year and has no health coverage already contributes over $2,400 a year to the system—enough for a healthy young adult to purchase a year's worth of health insurance.

The next two rows add in, for individuals and for families, the cost of employer-based health insurance. So, a household at the $50,000 income level with family health insurance coverage is paying over a quarter of its income into the health care system.

How were these figures derived? The tax component of the figures represents 34.4% of the total tax burden (federal, state, and local) on households at the three income levels. Of course, estimating average combined federal, state, and local taxes paid by households at different income levels is not a simple matter. The most comprehensive such estimates come from the Tax Foundation, a conservative think tank. Other analysts, however, including the liberal Center on Budget and Policy Priorities, view the Tax Foundation's figures as overestimating the total tax burden. The center has published its own estimates, based on figures from the Congressional Budget Office and Congress's Joint Committee on Taxation. The figures in the table are based on the CBO's numbers, which fall in between the Tax Foundation's estimates and the JCT-based estimates. (Estimates based on the Tax Foundation and JCT figures, along with details of the analysis, can be found at www.dollarsandsense.org.) It is worth noting that using the Tax Foundation's numbers, which show a larger share of income going to taxes at every income level, would have made the story even worse. For a family with health insurance earning $50,000 a year, for instance, the share of income going into health care would have been 28.7% rather than 26.4%.

For insurance premiums: in 2007, the average annual premiums for health insurance policies offered through employers were $4,479 for individuals and $12,106 for families, according to the Kaiser Family Foundation's annual survey of health benefits. Of course, some employers pay all or a large share of that premium while others pay half or less, leaving much of the premium cost to the worker. Either way, however, the full premium cost represents a bite taken out of the worker's total "wage packet"—the cost of wages plus benefits. This becomes evident when premiums go up: workers either see their own premium payments rise directly, or else face cuts or stagnation in their wages and non-health benefits. For that reason, economists typically view the entire premium as a cost imposed on the worker regardless of variations in employer contribution.

These figures are not meant to be exact, but do offer reasonable estimates of how much U.S. families are actually paying into the country's health care system today. Again, they do not include out-of-pocket expenses, which averaged 13.2% of all health care expenditures in 2005. Moreover, they do not include the risk of bankruptcy that health care costs impose: 50% of consumer bankruptcies in the United States stem from medical bills, including a surprising number among households that do have some kind of health coverage. Nor do they include the approximately 20% of auto insurance premiums or the 40% of workers' compensation premiums that pay for medical expenses.

Where Does All the Money Go?

After you've finished gasping in surprise at the share of your income that is already going into health care, you may wonder where all that money goes. One answer is that the United States has the most bureaucratic health care system in the world, including over 1,500 different companies, each offering multiple plans, each with its own marketing program and enrollment procedures, its own paperwork and policies, its CEO salaries, sales commissions, and other non-clinical costs—and, of course, if it is a for-profit company, its profits. Compared to the overhead costs of the single-payer approach, this fragmented system takes almost 25 cents more out of every health care dollar for expenses other than actually providing care.

Of the additional overhead in the current U.S. system, approximately half is borne by doctors' offices and hospitals, which are forced to maintain large billing and negotiating staffs to deal with all the plans. By contrast, under Canada's single-payer system (which is run by the provinces, not by the federal government), each medical specialty organization negotiates once a year with the nonprofit payer for each province to set fees, and doctors and hospitals need only bill that one payer.

Of course, the United States already has a universal, single-payer health care program: Medicare. Medicare, which serves the elderly and people with disabilities, operates with overhead costs equal to just 3% of total expenditures, compared to 15% to 25% overhead in private health programs. Since Medicare collects its revenue through the IRS, there is no need to collect from individuals, groups, or businesses. Some complexity remains—after all, Medicare must exist in the fragmented world that is American health care—but no matter how creative the opponents of single-payer get, there is no way they can show convincingly how the administrative costs of a single-payer system could come close to the current level.

Some opponents use current U.S. government expenditures for Medicare and Medicaid to arrive at frightening cost estimates for a universal single-payer health care system. They may use Medicare's $8,568 per person, or $34,272 for a family of four (2006). But they fail to mention that Medicare covers a very atypical, high-cost slice of the U.S. population: senior citizens, regardless of pre-existing conditions, and people with disabilities, including diagnoses such as AIDS and end-stage renal disease. Or they use Medicaid costs—forgetting to mention that half of Medicaid dollars pay for nursing homes, while the other half of Medicaid provides basic health care coverage, primarily to children in low-income households, at a cost of only about $1,500 a year per child.

Getting What We've Already Paid for

Americans spend more than anyone else in the world on health care. Each health insurer adds its bureaucracy, profits, high corporate salaries, advertising, and sales commissions to the actual cost of providing care. Not only is this money lost to health care, but it pays for a system that often makes it more difficult and complicated to receive the care we've already paid for. Shareholders are the primary clients of for-profit insurance companies, not patients.

Moreover, households' actual costs as a percentage of their incomes are far higher today than most imagine. Even families with no health insurance contribute substantially to our health care system through taxes. Recognizing the hidden costs that U.S. households pay for health care today makes it far easier to see how a universal single-payer system—with all of its obvious advantages—can cost most Americans less than the one we have today.

Joel A. Harrison, PhD, MPH, lives in San Diego, where he does consulting in epidemiology and research design. He has worked in the areas of preventive medicine, infectious diseases, medical outcomes research, and evidence-based clinical practice guidelines. He has lived and studied in both Canada and Sweden.

SOURCES: Center on Budget and Policy Priorities, "The Debate Over Tax Levels: How Much Does a Typical Family Pay?" March 11, 1998; Center on Budget and Policy Priorities, "Tax Foundation Figures Do Not Represent Middle-Income Tax Burdens: Figures May Mislead Policymakers, Journalists, and the Public," April 13, 2006; Center on Budget and Policy Priorities, "Clearing Up Confusion on the Cost of Covering Uninsured Children Eligible for Medicaid or SCHIP," March 13, 2007; Gary Claxton et al., "Health Benefits in 2007: Premium Increases Fall to an Eight-Year Low, While Offer Rates and Enrollment Remain Stable," Health Affairs 26(5), 2007 [based on "Employer Health Benefits 2007 Annual Survey" by the Kaiser Family Foundation]; Congressional Research Service, "U.S. Health Care Spending: Comparison with Other OECD Countries," September 17, 2007; Andrés de Francisco and Stephen Matlin, eds., Monitoring Financial Flows for Health Research 2006 (Global Forum for Health Research, 2006); Tax Foundation, "Who Pays America's Tax Burden, and Who Gets the Most Government Spending?" March 2007; Public Citizen Congress Watch, "Rx R&D Myths: The Case Against the Drug Industry's R&D 'Scare Card'," July 2001; Steffie Woolhandler et al., "Health Care Administration in the United States and Canada: Micromanagement, Macro Costs," Int'l Journal of Health Services 34(1), 2004; Steffie Woolhandler and David Himmelstein, "Paying for National Health Insurance—And Not Getting It," Health Affairs 21(4), July/August 2002.

Article 2
DON'T BLAME THE MINIMUM WAGE
An economist writes to a young woman who lost her job after the minimum wage was increased in her state.

PADDY QUICK
January/February 2008

Dear _____:

I'm so sorry you lost your job. I know how hard you worked and doubt very much that your employer was dissatisfied with your work. But I do not believe that the reason you lost your job was the increase in your state's minimum wage. Let me tell you why.

When businesses organize production, they figure out what different people they need to employ and in what numbers. A restaurant, for example, needs cooks, waiters/waitresses, dishwashers, cashiers and, sometimes, after-hours cleaning staff. It needs managers to keep track of who is doing what and when. Some of these people are paid a lot more than others, but they are all necessary. The lower-paid workers are as important as the higher-paid workers. Although the restaurant owner would like to pay them all less so that his profits would be higher, he needs them all.

This is important to understand. A bicycle needs two wheels, two pedals, a seat, a set of gears, and any number of parts that connect them all together. Which is most important? The front wheel? The rear wheel? The seat? The pedals? The fact that a pedal costs less than a wheel doesn't make it any less important. Similarly, all of the people who work in a restaurant play their part in the production of the meals you serve your customers, even though they "cost" their employer different amounts. If the pedal of a bicycle cost a bit more, it wouldn't be eliminated. Why then do you think your job would be eliminated if they had to pay you a little more?

People are laid off for many reasons. One possbilty is that employers just want to shuffle people around so that everyone feels under pressure. There are always a lot of people unemployed, and it is pretty easy to lay one person off and hire another to replace her. The new person is now likely to work harder than you did, even though you were doing a great job. There are also changes in the number of customers in different locations, and competition from other restaurants for these customers.

But you, I think, believe (or maybe you were told) that the higher wage the restaurant would have been required to pay you led to the elimination of your job. Understandably you might say that you would rather be paid the old wage and still have your job. But before you jump to the conclusion that they would have kept you on if only they hadn't had to raise your pay, think again about the bicycle pedal! How exactly can they replace you?

When the minimum wage increases, employers have to pay higher wages not only to those who received the old minimum, but also to those whose positions paid an extra dollar or more above that. If they decide to reorganize production, they may well decide to lay off these workers rather than the ones at the very bottom of the pay scale. Information technology, for example, may displace more highly paid workers who are responsible for inventory management at corporate headquarters, rather than the people like you who have direct contact with customers.

Corporations are, of course, always "crunching the numbers," figuring out whether they can save money by changing the combination of people and things they purchase in order to produce the pizzas and other things they sell. Sometimes they may be able to do so, but other times it may not be possible.

So let's look specifically at the fast food restaurant business to see the effect on employment of an increase in the minimum wage. It turns out that there isn't much that fast food restaurants can do when wages go up—other than hand over a small portion of their huge profits to their workforce!

Fast food corporations, such as McDonalds, spend millions lobbying Congress in opposition to a raise in minimum wage, pretending that their opposition has nothing to do with its effect on their profits. Instead they argue that it would break their hearts to have to lay off some of the poor people they employ. (Their employees are poor, of course, because of the low wages they receive!)

A famous study by two well-known economists, Alan Krueger of Princeton University and David Card of the University of California, Berkeley, looked very carefully at what happened to fast food employment in New Jersey in 1992 after that state raised its minimum wage. (This study is summarized in their 1997 book, *Myth and Measurement: The New Economics of the Minimum Wage*.) They compared New Jersey with its neighboring state, Pennsylvania, which did not raise its minimum wage. Fast food industry executives had argued that they would be "forced" to lay off workers if New Jersey raised its minimum wage, but the facts proved otherwise. New Jersey workers got higher wages, but they did *not* lose their jobs. So although it is *possible* that an increase in the minimum wage could lead restaurants to lay off workers, it turns out that this doesn't actually happen in the fast food industry.

After they studied minimum wages in the fast food industry, Krueger and Card went on to prove that increasing the minimum wage across the country as a whole has little or no effect on unemployment. This position was supported by a total of 650 economists, including five Nobel prize-winners, in a 2006 letter supporting the bill to raise the federal minimum wage to $7.15 an hour.

Production requires workers. Workers use tools and machinery, and businesses have the capital that is needed to buy these, but it is workers who turn the ovens, pizza dough, and tables into meals for their customers, and it is workers who make the computers that increasingly "mechanize" production. The big question, according to Adam Smith and other classical economists such as David Ricardo and Karl Marx, is how income is distributed, and in particular, how much of it goes to wage-earners.

Adam Smith, for example, believed that the level of wages depends on workers' bargaining power, and thought it obvious that the government was on the side of the employers. He did, however, think that if the rate of unemployment was low, wages could increase. Today, one part of the government, the Federal Reserve Board, takes this piece of theory very seriously, and makes sure that it keeps the rate of unemployment high enough to prevent wages from increasing! Smith's theory implies that we need to organize, both at the workplace and within the political system, to strengthen the power of labor against the power of capital.

Adam Smith also believed that wages could not sink below the minimum needed for workers to survive and bring up children. But unfortunately, when there is a lot of unemployment, workers find themselves in a "race to the bottom": "I'll work for whatever you're willing to pay me." "No, take me. I'll work for $1 less." "Please, please, I'll work for food." During the Great Depression, massive unemployment made this a terrifying possibility, and led to the enactment of minimum wage legislation. This was an important victory for an organized working class. But it is an ongoing struggle. With a decent minimum wage and low unemployment, we can get the higher wages that our hard work entitles us to.

I wish you every success in your search for a new job. I expect when you find it you will earn more than you did before, thanks to your state's increase in the minimum wage.

Love, Paddy

Paddy Quick teaches economics at St. Francis College, Brooklyn.

SOURCES: David Card & Alan B. Krueger, *Myth and Measurement: The New Economics of the Minimum Wage*, Princeton University Press, 1997; Adam Smith, *Wealth of Nations*, 1776 (Part I, Ch. 8).

Article 3
INEQUALITY: BAD FOR YOUR HEALTH
An Interview with Social Epidemiologist Ichiro Kawachi

January/February 2008

How do you stay healthy? That's a no brainer, right? Eat the right foods, exercise, quit smoking, get regular medical checkups. Epidemiologist Ichiro Kawachi wants to add a new item to the list: live in a relatively egalitarian society. Kawachi, a professor of social epidemiology at the Harvard School of Public Health, has carried out a wide range of research studies on the social and economic factors that account for average health outcomes in different societies. Among the most novel conclusions of this body of research is that people in soci-eties with high levels of economic inequality are less healthy than those living in more equal societies, regardless of their absolute levels of income.

Health policy is at least on the table in this election year. The conversation, however, is almost entirely limited to whether and how to ensure universal health insurance coverage. The work of Kawachi and his colleagues suggests that the public debate about health really needs to be much broader, encompassing a wide range of public policies—in many cases economic policies—that do not explicitly address health but that nonetheless condition how long and how robust our lives will be. Their work traces the multidimensional connection between an individual's health and the qualities of her social world, many of

which can shift dramatically when the gap between rich and poor widens.
  Kawachi spoke with Dollars & Sense in November 2007.

DOLLARS & SENSE: Your research looks at the relationship between economic factors and health, especially whether living in a more unequal society, in itself, has a negative effect on health outcomes—and you have found evidence that it does. But I want to start by being really clear about what this hypothesis means. There seems to be such a complicated web of possible relationships between income and health.

ICHIRO KAWACHI: Let's start with how your own income affects your health. Most obviously, income enables people to purchase the goods and services that promote health: purchasing good, healthy food, being able to use the income to live in a safe and healthy neighborhood, being able to purchase sports equipment. Income enables people to carry out the advice of public health experts about how to behave in ways that promote longevity.

But in addition to that, having a secure income has an important psychosocial effect. It provides people with a sense of control and mastery over their lives. And lots of psychologists now say that sense of control, along with the ability to plan for the future, is in itself a very important source of psychological health. Knowing that your future is secure, that you're not going to be too financially stressed, also provides incentives for people to invest in their health. Put another way, if my mind is taken up with having to try to make ends meet, I don't have sufficient time to listen to my doctor's advice and invest in my health in various ways.

So there are some obvious ways in which having adequate income is important for health. This is what we call the absolute income effect—that is, the effect of your own income on your own health. If only absolute income matters, then your health is determined by your income alone, and it doesn't matter what anybody else makes. But our hypothesis has been that relative income might also matter: namely, where your income stands in relation to others'. That's where the distribution of income comes in. We have looked at the idea that when the distance between your income and the incomes of the rest of society grows very large, this may pose an additional health hazard.

D&S: How could people's relative income have an impact on health, even if their incomes are adequate in absolute terms?

IK: There are a couple of possible pathways. One is this ancient theory of relative deprivation: the idea that given a particular level of income, the greater the distance between your income and the incomes of the rest of society, the more miserable you feel. People are sensitive to their relative position in society vis-à-vis income. You may have a standard of living above the poverty level; nonetheless, if you live in a community or a society in which everyone else is making so much more, you might feel frustrated or miserable as a result, and this might have deleterious psychological and perhaps behavioral consequences. So that's one idea.

Another hypothesis about why income distribution matters is that when the income or wealth gap between the top and bottom grows, certain things begin to happen within the realm of politics. For example, when the wealthiest segment of society pulls away from the rest of us, they literally begin to segregate themselves in terms of where they live, and they begin to purchase services like health care and education through private means. This translates into a dynamic where wealthy people see that their tax dollars are not being spent for their own benefit, which in turn leads to a reduced basis for cooperation and spending on public goods. So I think there is an entirely separate political mechanism that's distinct from the psychological mechanism involved in notions of relative deprivation. These are some of the key ways in which income inequality is corrosive for the public's health.

D&S: When you talk about relative deprivation, are you talking primarily about poor people, or does the evidence suggest that inequality affects health outcomes up and down the income ladder? For instance, what about the middle class? I think for the public to understand the inequality effect as something different from just the absolute-income effect, they would have to see that it isn't only poor people who can be hurt by inequality.

IK: Exactly, that's my argument. If you subscribe to the theory that it's only your own income that matters for health, then obviously middle-class people would not have much to worry about—they're able to put food on the table, they have adequate clothing and shelter, they're beyond poverty. What the relative-income theory suggests is that even middle-class people might be less healthy than they would be if they lived in a more egalitarian society.

D&S: That's what I was wondering about. Say we compared a person at the median income level in the United States versus Germany, both of whom certainly have enough income to cover all of the basic building blocks of good health. Would this hypothesis lead you to expect that, other things being equal, the middle-income person in the United States will likely have worse health because economic inequality is greater here?

IK: Yes, that's exactly right. And that's borne out. Americans are much less healthy than Europeans, for example, in spite of having higher average wealth.

D&S: But, unlike most other rich countries, the United States does not have universal health care. Couldn't that explain the poorer health outcomes here?

IK: Not entirely. There was a very interesting paper that came out last year comparing the health of Americans to the health of people in England, using very comparable, nationally representative surveys. They looked at the prevalence of major conditions such as heart attack, obesity, diabetes, hypertension. On virtually every indicator, the top third of Americans by income—virtually all of whom had health insurance—were still sicker than the bottom third of people in England. The comparison was confined to white Americans and white Britons, so they even abstracted out the contribution of racial disparities.

Health insurance certainly matters—I'm not downgrading its importance—

but part of the reason Americans are so sick is because we live in a really unequal society, and it begins to tell on the physiology.

D&S: Has anyone tried to compare countries that have universal health care but have differing levels of inequality?

IK: There have been comparisons across Western European countries, all of which pretty much have universal coverage. If you compare the Scandinavian countries against the U.K. and other European countries, you generally see that the Scandinavians do have a better level of health. The more egalitarian the country, the healthier its citizens tend to be. But that's about as much as we can say. I'm not aware of really careful comparative studies; I'm making a generalization based on broad patterns.

D&S: It sounds like there is still plenty of research to do.

IK: Yes.

D&S: You have already mentioned a couple of possible mechanisms by which an unequal distribution of income could affect health. Are there any other mechanisms that you would point to?

IK: I think those are the two big ones: the political mechanism, which happens at the level of society when the income distribution widens, and then the individual mechanism, which is the relative deprivation that people feel. But I should add that relative deprivation itself can affect health through a variety of mechanisms. For instance, there is evidence that a sense of relative deprivation leads people into a spending race to try to keep up with the Joneses—a pattern of conspicuous, wasteful consumption, working in order to spend, to try to keep up with the lifestyle of the people at the top. This leads to many behaviors with deleterious health consequences, among them overwork, stress, not spending enough time with loved ones, and so forth.

Very interestingly, a couple of economists recently analyzed a study of relative deprivation, which used an index based upon the gap between your income and the incomes of everybody above you within your social comparison group, namely, people with the same occupation, or people in the same age group or living in the same state. What they found was that the greater the gap between a person's own income and the average income of their comparison group, the shorter their lives, the lower their life expectancy, as well as the higher their smoking rates, the higher their utilization of mental health services, and so on. This is suggestive evidence that deprivation relative to average income may actually matter for people's health.

D&S: It's interesting—this part of your analysis almost starts to dovetail with Juliet Schor's work.

IK: Absolutely, that's right. What Juliet Schor writes about in The Overspent American is consumerism. It seems to me that in a society with greater income inequality, there's so much more consumerism, that the kind of pathological behavior she describes is so much more acute in unequal societies, driven by people trying to emulate the behavior of those who are pulling away from them.

D&S: Your research no doubt reflects your background as a social epidemiologist. However, it seems as though many mainstream economists view these issues completely differently: many do not accept the existence of any causal effect running from income to health, except possibly to the degree that your income affects how much health care you can purchase.

IK: Yes, there is a lot of pushback from economists who, as you say, are even skeptical that absolute income matters for health. What I would say to them is, try to be a little bit open-minded about the empirical evidence. It seems to me that much of the dismissal from economists is not based upon looking at the empirical data. When they do, there is a shift: some economists are now beginning to publish studies that actually agree with what we are saying. For example, the study on relative deprivation and health I mentioned was done by a couple of economists.

Another example: some studies by an erstwhile critic of mine, Jeffrey Milyo, and Jennifer Mellor, who in the past have criticized our studies on income distribution and health in the United States as not being robust to different kinds of model specifications—a very technical debate. Anyway, most recently they published an interesting study based on an experiment in which they had participants play a prisoners' dilemma kind of game to see how much they cooperate as opposed to act selfishly. One of the things Mellor and Milyo found was that as they varied the distribution of the honoraria they paid to the participants, the more unequal the distribution of this "income," the more selfishly the players acted. They concluded that their results support what we have been contending, which is that income inequality leads to psychosocial effects where people become less trusting, less cohesive, and less likely to contribute to public spending.

D&S: That's fascinating.

IK: Yes, it's very interesting. So watch this space, because some of the recent evidence from economists themselves has begun to support what we're saying.

D&S: In other parts of the world, and especially in Africa, there are examples of societies whose economies are failing or stagnating because of widespread public health issues, for example HIV/AIDS. So it seems as if not only can low income cause poor health, but also that poor health can cause low income. I wonder if your research has anything to say about the complicated web between income and health that those countries are dealing with.

IK: There's no doubt that in sub-Saharan Africa, poor health is the major impediment to economic growth. You have good econometric studies suggesting that the toll of HIV, TB, and malaria alone probably slows economic growth by a measurable amount, maybe 1½ percentage points per year. So there's no question that what those countries need is investment to improve people's health, in order for them to even begin thinking about escaping the poverty trap.

The same is true in the United States, by the way. Although I've told the story in which the direction of causation runs from income to health, of course poor health is also a major cause of loss of income. When people become ill, for example, they can lose their jobs and hence their income.

What I'll say about the developing world is that in many ways, the continuing lack of improvement in health in, for example, sub-Saharan Africa is itself an expression of the maldistribution of income in the world. As you know, the rich countries are persistently failing to meet the modest amount of funding that's being asked by the World Health Organization to solve many of these problems, like providing malaria tablets and bed nets and HIV pills for everyone in sub-Saharan Africa. If you look at inequality on a global scale, the world itself could benefit from some more redistribution. Today the top 1% of the world's population owns about a third of the world's wealth. So, although certainly the origins of the HIV epidemic are not directly related to income inequality, I think the solution lies in redistributing wealth and income through overseas development aid, from the 5% of the world who live in the rich countries to everyone else.

D&S: Leaving aside some of the countries with the most devastating public health problems, poor countries in general are often focused just on economic growth, on getting their per capita GDP up, but this often means that inequality increases as well—like in China. Do you view the inequality effect as significant enough that a developing country concerned about its health outcomes should aim to limit the growth of inequality even if that meant sacrificing some economic growth?

IK: It depends on the country's objectives. But I'd ask the question: what is the purpose of economic growth if not to assure people's level of well-being, which includes their health? Why do people care about economic growth? In order to lead a satisfying and long life, many people would say. If that's the case, then many people living in developing countries may feel exactly as you suggest: they would prefer policies that attend to egalitarian distribution over policies that are aimed purely at growth.

Amartya Sen has written about this; he has pointed to many countries that are poor but nonetheless enjoy a very good level of health. He cites examples like Costa Rica and the Kerala region in India, which are much, much poorer than the United States but enjoy a high level of health. It really depends on the objectives of the country's politicians. In Kerala and Costa Rica, their health record is very much a reflection of how their governments have invested their income in areas that promote health, like education and basic health services—even if doing so means causing a bit of a drag on economic growth.

China also had this record until perhaps ten years ago. Now they're in this era of maximizing growth, and we're seeing a very steep rise in inequality. Although we don't have good health statistics from China, my guess is that this is probably going to tell on its national health status. Actually, we already know that improvement in their child mortality rates for children under five has begun to slow down in the last

20 years, since the introduction of their economic reforms. In the 1950s and 1960s, the records seemed to suggest quite rapid improvements in health in China. But that's begun to slow down.

D&S: Certainly your research on the health effects of inequality could represent a real challenge in the United States in terms of health care policy. In many ways we have a very advanced health care system, but many people are not well served by it. What effect do you think your work could or should have on U.S. health policy?

IK: Regardless of whether you believe what I'm saying about income inequality, the most basic interpretation of this research is that there are many things that determine people's health besides simply access to good health services. We spend a lot of time discussing how to improve health insurance coverage in this country. In the current presidential debates, when they talk about health policy, they're mostly talking about health insurance. But it's myopic to confine discussions of health policy to what's going to be done about health insurance. There are many social determinants of health and thus many other policy options for improving Americans' health. Investing in education, reducing the disparities in income, attacking problems of poverty, improving housing for poor people, investing in neighborhood services and amenities—these are all actually health policies. The most fundamental point about this whole area of research is that there are many determinants of health besides what the politicians call health policy.

D&S: Besides doctors and medical care.

IK: Yes, that's right. I used to be a physician, and physicians do a lot of good, but much of health is also shaped by what goes on outside the health care system. That's probably the most important thing.

The second thing is the implication that income certainly matters for health. So policies that affect peoples' incomes, both absolute and relative income, may have health consequences. For instance, I think the kinds of tax policies we have had in recent years—where most of the benefits have accrued to the top 1% and the resulting budget deficits have led to cutbacks of services to the rest of us, especially those in the bottom half of the income distribution—have been a net negative for public health, through the kind of political mechanism I have described.

D&S: It's almost as though there should be a line for health care in the cost-benefit analysis of any change in tax policies or other economic policies.

IK: Absolutely. There's an idea in public health called the health impact assessment. It's a technique modeled after environmental impact assessments, a set of tools that people are advocating should be used at the Cabinet level. The idea is that when, say, the treasury secretary suggests some new economic measure, then we can formally put the proposal through a modeling exercise to forecast its likely effects on health. Health certainly is very sensitive to decisions that are made elsewhere in the Cabinet besides what goes on in Health and Human Services.

D&S: What about global health policy? Are groups like the World Health Organization paying attention to the kind of research that you do?

IK: Yes, they are. Maybe seven or eight years ago, the WHO had a commission on macroeconomics and health, headed by Jeffrey Sachs. The idea was, by increasing funding to tackle big health problems in the developing world, we can also improve their economic performance and end poverty. That commission posed the direction of causality from health to income. In the last three years, the WHO has had a new commission on the social determinants of health, headed by a social epidemiologist from England, Michael Marmot. That group is looking at the other direction of causality—namely, from poverty to ill health—and considering the ways in which government policies in different areas can improve people's social environment in order to improve their health. I think they are due to report next year with some recommendations as well as case examples from different countries, mostly developing countries whose governments have tried to tackle the economic side of things in order to improve health outcomes.

D&S: Right now the United States is continuing on this path of becoming more and more economically stratified. Your work suggests that that doesn't bode well for us in terms of health. I wonder—this is very speculative—but if we stay on this path of worsening inequality, what do you predict our health as a country is likely to look like in 20 or 30 years?

IK: We're already in the bottom third of the 23 OECD countries, the rich countries, in terms of our average health status. Most people are dimly aware that we spend over half of the medical dollars expended on this planet, so they assume that we should therefore be able to purchase the highest level of health. I teach a course on social determinants of health at Harvard, and many of my students are astonished to discover that America is not number one in life expectancy.

I predict that if we continue on this course of growing income inequality, we will continue to slip further. That gains in life expectancy will continue to slow down. Life expectancy is increasing every year, probably because of medical advances, but I suspect that eventually there will be a limit to how much can be delivered through high-tech care and that our health will slip both in relative terms, compared to the rest of the OECD countries, and maybe even in absolute terms, losing some of the gains we have had over the last half century. For example, some demographers are already forecasting that life expectancy will drop in the coming century because of the obesity epidemic. Add that to the possible effects of income inequality, and I could easily imagine a scenario in which life expectancy might decline in absolute terms as well as in relative terms. It's likely that we have not yet seen the full impact of the recent rise in inequality on health status, because it takes a while for the full health effects to become apparent in the population.

The interview was conducted by D&S co-editor Amy Gluckman and intern Alissa Thuotte.

Article 4
COMPARATIVE ADVANTAGE
RAMAA VASUDEVAN
July/August 2007

Dear Dr. Dollar:
When economists argue that the outsourcing of jobs might be a plus for the U.S. economy, they often mention the idea of comparative advantage. So free trade would allow the United States to specialize in higher-end service-sector businesses, creating higher-paying jobs than the ones that would be outsourced. But is it really true that free trade leads to universal benefits?
—David Goodman, Boston, Mass.

You're right: The purveyors of the free trade gospel do invoke the doctrine of comparative advantage to dismiss widespread concerns about the export of jobs. Attributed to 19th-century British political-economist David Ricardo, the doctrine says that a nation always stands to gain if it exports the goods it produces relatively more cheaply in exchange for goods that it can get comparatively more cheaply from abroad. Free trade would lead to each country specializing in the products it can produce at relatively lower costs. Such specialization allows both trading partners to gain from trade, the theory goes, even if in one of the countries production of both goods costs more in absolute terms.

For instance, suppose that in the United States the cost to produce one car equals the cost to produce 10 bags of cotton, while in the Philippines the cost to produce one car equals the cost to produce 100 bags of cotton. The Philippines would then have a comparative advantage in the production of cotton, producing one bag at a cost equal to the production cost of 1/100 of a car, versus 1/10 of a car in the United States; likewise, the United States would hold a comparative advantage in the production of cars. Whatever the prices of cars and cotton in the global market, the theory goes, the Philippines would be better off producing only cotton and importing all its cars from the United States, and the United States would be better off producing only cars and importing all of its cotton from the Philippines. If the international terms of trade—the relative price—is one car for 50 bags, then the United States will take in 50 bags of cotton for each car it exports, 40 more than the 10 bags it forgoes by putting its productive resources into making the car rather than growing cotton. The Philippines is also better off: it can import a car in exchange for the export of 50 bags of cotton, whereas it would have had to forgo the production of 100 bags of cotton in order to produce that car domestically. If the price of cars goes up in the global marketplace, the Philippines will lose out in relative terms—but will still be better off than if it tried to produce its own cars.

The real world, unfortunately, does not always conform to the assumptions underlying comparative-advantage theory. One assumption is that trade is balanced. But many countries are running persistent deficits, notably the United States, whose trade deficit is now at nearly 7% of its GDP. A second premise, that there is full employment within the trading nations, is also patently unrealistic. As global trade intensifies, jobs created in the export sector do not necessarily compensate for the jobs lost in the sectors wiped out by foreign competition.

The comparative advantage story faces more direct empirical challenges as well. Nearly 70% of U.S. trade is trade in similar goods, known as intra-industry trade: for example, exporting Fords and importing BMWs. And about one third of U.S. trade as of the late 1990s was trade between branches of a single corporation located in different countries (intra-firm trade). Comparative advantage cannot explain these patterns.

Comparative advantage is a static concept that identifies immediate gains from trade but is a poor guide to economic development, a process of structural change over time which is by definition dynamic. Thus the comparative advantage tale is particularly pernicious when preached to developing countries, consigning many to "specialize" in agricultural goods or be forced into a race to the bottom where cheap sweatshop labor is their sole source of competitiveness.

The irony, of course, is that none of the rich countries got that way by following the maxim that they now preach. These countries historically relied on tariff walls and other forms of protectionism to build their industrial base. And even now, they continue to protect sectors like agriculture with subsidies. The countries now touted as new models of the benefits of free trade—South Korea and the other "Asian tigers," for instance—actually flouted this economic wisdom, nurturing their technological capabilities in specific manufacturing sectors and taking advantage of their lower wage costs to gradually become effective competitors of the United States and Europe in manufacturing.

The fundamental point is this: contrary to the comparative-advantage claim that trade is universally beneficial, nations as a whole do not prosper from free trade. Free trade creates winners and losers, both within and between countries. In today's context it is the global corporate giants that are propelling and profiting from "free trade": not only outsourcing white-collar jobs, but creating global commodity chains linking sweatshop labor in the developing countries of Latin America and Asia (Africa being largely left out of the game aside from the export of natural resources such as oil) with ever-more insecure consumers in the developed world. Promoting "free trade" as a political cause enables this process to continue.

It is a process with real human costs in terms of both wages and work. People in developing countries across the globe continue to face these costs as trade liberalization measures are enforced; and the working class in the United States is also being forced to bear the brunt of the relentless logic of competition.

Ramaa Vasudevan teaches economics at Barnard College and is on the D&S collective.

RESOURCES: Arthur MacEwan, "The Gospel of Free Trade: The New Evangelists," *Dollars & Sense*, July/August 2002; Ha-Joon Chang, *Kicking away the Ladder: The Real History of Fair Trade*, Foreign Policy in Focus, 2003; Anwar Shaikh, "Globalization and the Myths of Free Trade," in *Globalization and the Myths of Free Trade: History, Theory, and Empirical Evidence*, ed. Anwar Shaikh, Routledge 2007.

Article 5

THE CARE GAP
Why we ignore those in need, and what to do about it.

ROBERT DRAGO
Spring 2007

Work-family conflict is usually portrayed as a middle class, white woman's problem: how can you balance a demanding career with raising your children? This problem is indeed daunting, but if we want to understand the true costs of work-family conflict, we also need to ask whether those who need care—disabled adults and elders as well as children—are receiving it. If many are not, then we confront a care gap that we as a society should strive to close—and that cannot be closed apart from addressing the underlying causes of the imbalance that so many people in the United States struggle with today.

The care gap—the number of people who are receiving adequate care subtracted from the total who need it—is difficult to measure accurately, both because much of the care work performed in our society is unpaid and invisible, and for the more prosaic reason that no national survey has provided good direct measures of care adequacy. Yet only by measuring the care gap can we can gauge the success of attempts to close it. Although difficult, it *is* possible to estimate the overall care gap with available data, by using proxy measures for the adequacy of care. And it turns out to be large.

Who Needs Care?

This seemingly innocuous question is difficult to answer in practice. It seems safe to classify children under the age of, say, 16, as needing care. We might classify the elderly as needing care as well; however, a substantial proportion of older Americans are living healthy, independent lives. Disability—including severe vision or hearing impairment as well as other conditions that substantially limit one or more basic physical activities—is a better indicator of whether an adult needs care. Admittedly, some disabilities may allow for substantial independence. However, recent data from the American Community Survey conducted by the Census Bureau suggest that people with disabilities typically do need care. For example, among 16- to 64-year-olds, over 21 million people report disabilities. More than half of this group (12.3 million) report related employment difficulties, and an overlapping 5.2 million report difficulty going outside the home. Among the 13.5 million people 65 years and older with disabilities, more than 5.5 million report difficulty going outside of the home, while an overlapping 3 million-plus report self-care problems.

Combining people under 16 and adults and elders with disabilities produces the totals in the bottom row of Table 1. In 2004, almost 100 million people out of 284 million, or 34.9% of the U.S. population, needed care on a regular basis. The care-dependent are concentrated in high and low age groups: more than three-quarters of all those who need care are either below the age of 16 or above the age of 64.

After shrinking slightly in recent decades, the care-dependent population is beginning to grow. Children aren't driving the shift—the percentage of young children is projected to fall slightly from around 6.8% of the population to 6.7% by 2010. However, those over 75 are projected to rise from just under 6% to around 8% of the population over the course of the current decade alone, according to U.S. Department of Commerce data. Even more dramatic growth in the elderly population looms on the horizon.

Who Gets Care?

To estimate the size of the care gap, we need to know how many people are getting adequate care. The term "adequate care" is of course ambiguous, and there are no direct measures. But several indicators, including poverty rates and an alternative measure of poverty, as well as estimates of the provision and quality of child and elder care, can allow us to at least begin to gauge the size of the care gap.

Poverty rates are a decent proxy for lack of adequate care insofar as poverty limits caregivers' ability to provide such resources as food, shelter, and health care. Despite a variety of anti-poverty programs, the United States' safety net is so porous that poor children remain more likely to go hungry, to suffer from various diseases, and to have no regular health insurance than nonpoor children (see "Does Poverty Mean Poor Care?" p. 32). In a 2005 study of mothers with family incomes below 200% of the poverty line, sociologists Lisa Dodson and Ellen Bravo documented the enormous strains that low incomes place on parents' ability to care for their children: almost half of the mothers had no access to a car, many of their children worried about whether there would be food on the table or whether they would become homeless, the employed mothers worried constantly about their child care arrangements, and the mothers often lost their jobs because they had to care for sick children. No matter how hard these women work on the job or at home, and even though many frequently shortchange themselves on sleep, they cannot always prevent their children from falling into the care gap; they simply lack the resources to provide adequate care.

Our social safety net is likewise extremely porous for adults with disabilities. For instance, adults who experience disability due to an injury at work are eligible for Medicare after 29 months, but their odds of dying rise almost tenfold during the waiting period because they often lack health insurance coverage.

Poverty rates by age group, gender, and disability are summarized in Table 2. (The table does not include figures for children under five, who are added back in below.) The table reveals that poverty is associated with youth: children exhibit the highest rates regardless of gender or disability status. Conversely, the elderly exhibit low rates of poverty, largely thanks to Social Security. Rates of poverty are markedly higher for women and girls in every category. Finally, poverty rates are consistently higher among the disabled. Thought of as probabilities, the odds of a non-disabled man over the age of 64 living in poverty are just over one in 20 (5.3%). In contrast, for a nondisabled woman over 64, the odds of living in poverty are closer to one in 10 (8.6%). And a girl in her early teens with a disability is more than five times more likely to be living in poverty than a non-disabled elderly man.

Separate estimates from the Census Bureau suggest that 20.5% of all children under the age of five were living in poverty in the year 2004. (The Census Bureau figures are not broken down by disability status and so are not reported in Table 2.) Adding this figure to those in Table 2 shows that 19% of those needing care live in poverty, compared to only 9.9% of those who do not need care. *Those who need care in our society are around twice as likely to live in poverty as those who do not.* Moreover, *over half of all individuals currently living in poverty either are children or have a disability.*

As disturbing as this is, the official poverty level is actually far too low to capture income levels most Americans would consider even barely adequate. Specifically, the level may be set below what is needed to provide care, leading us to underestimate the care gap. Researchers at the Economic Policy Institute propose an alternative poverty indicator, based on a basic family budget, that accounts for increases in rents as well as for expenses not included in the official rate, such as health insurance and telephones. Most of us don't think of a telephone as a luxury, particularly if it is a single landline, and health insurance is part of any conception of an adequate standard of care. This alternative benchmark shows that official statistics underestimate the percentage of families with children living in poverty by approximately 150%.

The extent of underestimation is likely even more severe among those needing care; since a disproportionate number in this group fall below the official poverty line, many in need of care are likely hovering just above it. So it is reasonably conservative to estimate that the share of the population needing care but with insufficient incomes is 150% greater than the official poverty figures suggest. According to this alternative calculation, at least 47.5% of those who need care live in a household that cannot afford such basic necessities as health insurance or quality child or elder care. Looked at differently, 16.6% of the overall population is subject to a care gap in which a need for care coincides with insufficient income.

Care involves more than just money, and the care gap affects even middle- and high-income families. For example, while higher-income families can afford to pay the substantial fees for center-based care for children or for a nursing home placement for an elderly parent, the quality of care in these settings can be unacceptably low.

Parents find low quality pervasive in child care centers. A 1999 report on the quality of child care in the United States from the National Council of Jewish Women found a full 80% of child care centers are mediocre to poor and that staff turnover averages more than 30% per year. Such high turnover is disturbing because it means our youngest children often wake up in the morning not knowing who will care for them during much of the day. It also means care providers frequently have little knowledge of a child's specific needs.

For older children, after-school programs have become a needed alternative to spending their afternoon hours alone and unsupervised—as well as a way to enhance their educational opportunities. Here quality is not so much an issue as quantity. A 2002-2003 study by the Afterschool Alliance estimated that while 6.5 million children from grades kindergarten through 12 are enrolled in after-school programs, an additional 15 million youth would enroll if the programs existed and were affordable.

At the other end of the age spectrum is elder care, where a recent government-funded report suggests quality is no better in nursing homes than in child care centers. The report, by Abt Associates, found 90% of nursing homes have staffing levels so low that they create dangerous conditions for those who live there.

For people with disabilities across the age spectrum, we have no comparable figures to help us assess the quality of care they receive, in part because their care needs are so varied. Nonetheless, there is no reason to believe that the disabled are subject to significantly higher standards of care than children or the elderly.

We know that poverty afflicts over 47% of those in need of care. Beyond this economic indicator of the care gap, we also know that the vast majority of child care centers and nursing homes are of poor quality and that there is a significant shortage of after-school programs. These findings suggest that the 47% figure underestimates—perhaps significantly—the shortfall of quality care for those in need. A very cautious estimate, then, is that *the care gap affects over half of those in need of care.* With 34.9% of the population estimated to need care, the care gap affects at least 17.5%. Almost one out of five Americans—around 50 million people all told—need care but are receiving inadequate care or no care at all.

The figure above illustrates the care gap. Many in the overall population, the largest circle, do not need care. Those needing care are on the inside left circle, while those who are poor fall into the right circle, with the overlap representing the care gap. We should be shrinking that gap, but instead we are allowing it to expand. Between 2000 and 2005, the number of U.S. residents living in poverty grew by five and a half million or by 1.3% of the entire population while, as mentioned earlier, the number of elderly needing care will continue to rise for the foreseeable future.

In the wealthiest nation in the history of the planet, it should be a source of great shame that we do not care for most of those in need within our own borders. We could, and should, rectify this situation. Moreover, the search for balance is intimately connected to the care gap. Most adults will not be able to achieve balance in their lives unless and until the care gap is closed. A single mother facing difficulties putting food on the table cannot achieve balance, and neither can a high-paid professional who has to leave his children alone and unsupervised. We all suffer from the care gap.

Why Is There a Care Gap?

It is tempting to trace the source of the care gap to the Bush administration. After all, if the administration were willing to provide adequate supports for families and individuals with disabilities, the care gap would largely disappear. While that is true, it ignores the deeper question of why we as a society permitted a care gap to emerge in recent decades, and the current administration surely cannot be held accountable for all of that. Instead, I attribute the care gap to deeply seated norms around motherhood, ideal workers, and individualism.

Norms are broad rules of behavior that govern our expectations of others and of ourselves, and that carry penalties for those who deviate from them. Like customs, norms help us make sense of situations and reach quick decisions. Driving on the right side of the road is a custom in the United States that facilitates safe driving. Norms, however, run deeper than customs. We often use norms to guide our responses to genuinely new circumstances, even when our values point in other directions.

Three norms, I believe, help explain the care gap. These norms are:

- *The Motherhood norm*—a society-wide belief that women should be mothers *and* should provide the care that family members and others need for little or no pay.
- *The Ideal Worker norm*—a belief among managers and professionals in total commitment to career, and high rewards for that behavior.
- *The Individualism norm*—a society-wide belief that people ought to be self-reliant and that the government should not help those needing care.

How do these norms operate? Consider a nurse at an elementary school examining a feverish child; she needs to decide which parent to call to take the child home. Even if mom and dad are both employed during the school day, the norm of motherhood tells us that mom is more likely to get the call.

The norm of motherhood leads women to expect, and be expected, to serve as caregivers for their families and, more broadly, to care for anyone in need, and to do so for love rather than money. Most centrally, the norm leads us to anticipate that women will become biological mothers and care for their children, and also implies that girls and women themselves hold these expectations. The school nurse who calls mom is not just acting on a stereotype; the norm of motherhood implies that the mother, and perhaps even the child, would feel slighted if dad got the call instead.

We can get a glimpse of the ideal worker norm in the results of focus groups I helped conduct with seniors in the hotel and restaurant management program at Penn State University. We asked the students how they would handle child care responsibilities if they became parents. Few of the students had thought about it. Pressed as to why, it turned out that most planned to wait 10 to 15 years before having children. These young people, with seemingly boundless energy and enthusiasm, believed their careers would initially demand too much effort and travel, and would involve hours that are too unpredictable, to add a child to the equation. They also believed these extreme demands would eventually diminish, leaving time for family commitments.

These students understood the ideal worker norm as a set of expectations that would be placed upon them during the early stages of their careers. What they failed to understand is that many of them will likely work long hours into their 40s and 50s, and that these hours will be largely self-imposed.

The ideal worker norm is not applied equally to everyone. Employees in non-professional or non-managerial occupations are rarely expected to exhibit high levels of commitment. The norm largely serves as a dividing line within the workforce, segmenting off those who strive to be worthy and committed to meeting the demands of the norm from those who are unworthy and not expected to adhere to them. However, this line can be crossed quite easily, at least in a downward direction, and particularly by women. For example, in many professional workplaces, if a man announces that a new baby is on the way, he is typically congratulated. A woman making the same announcement may be similarly congratulated, but she will also likely be asked, "How soon are you going part-time?" The presumption that she will no longer seek to function as an ideal worker—because of the motherhood norm—means that she has crossed this particular line with a few simple words.

The third norm, of individualism, results in a belief that the government cannot and should not be responsible for taking care of those who are unable to care for themselves due to age or disability. While the current administration epitomizes this belief, the individualism norm was equally in play when President Clinton signed welfare reform legislation in 1996. The legislation was, in the president's famous phrase, intended to "end welfare as we know it" by removing financial supports for single mothers and their children and replacing them with resources to help poor moms obtain and hold jobs. The legislation enshrined the idea that the government should not be in the business of helping people.

The norm of individualism unquestionably lies behind the care gap: as mentioned earlier, if enough government resources were devoted to the direct provision of care, and to providing parents and other caregivers with sufficient income and time for their families, the care gap could be closed.

But that analysis misses the effects of the other two norms. The motherhood norm allows our society to ignore the care gap by expecting women to deal with it out of the goodness of their hearts, and with low or no expectation of financial returns. The norm of the ideal worker makes it impossible for many men, and an increasing number of women, to have sufficient time for family or other care commitments. Even in a two-parent family, both parents typically hold down jobs, leaving little time for the unpaid work involved in raising children or caring for elderly or disabled relatives. The norm of individualism is not the only cause of the care gap.

Closing the Gap

Why do norms matter for efforts to close the care gap? Policy initiatives alone, whether related to government, employers, or unions and community groups, will generally be insufficient to close the gap unless the three norms I've discussed are challenged more directly. More to the point, unless we challenge the three norms, we will lack the political will to close the care gap.

So how do we challenge norms? Consider the increasing amount of work that fathers are doing in the home. This change came about because couples negotiated the division of domestic labor. By moving couples beyond the constricting norms of motherhood and the ideal worker, such negotiations made it easier and more acceptable for men to make a greater contribution in the home. Negotiations between mothers and fathers led to fairer outcomes because women demanded greater equality in the home.

Such negotiations can take place in other settings as well. Taking a page from efforts to enhance cultural diversity, researchers and practitioners are increasingly honing in on practices and programs that create so-called "inclusive environments." An inclusive environment is one in which the diverse needs of all are systematically brought to the surface and discussed. Norms place blinders over our eyes, but inclusive processes offer hope for removing those blinders, permitting us to make our values explicit and achieve improvements through negotiation and compromise.

While inclusive processes are by no means common in U.S. workplaces today, there are plenty of real-world examples. For instance, I have studied workgroups that schedule their own working time and create space in the workday for doctors' appointments or for parents to be absent when schools have snow days. At the organizational level, unions such as HERE Local 2 in San Francisco, whose members are hotel workers, have improved supports for families in a low-wage environment in unique ways that the members themselves designed. And at the community level, partnerships are bringing together schools, government agencies, unions, employers, and nonprofit groups to improve the quality and affordability of child care. In each of these cases, because diverse needs are voiced and prioritized, norms are challenged as our conscious values—in particular, the value of caring for children and for people with disabilities—come to the forefront. Because inclusive processes give voice to our needs, hopes, and dreams, they facilitate compromises beyond the limited set of outcomes dictated by longstanding norms.

Public supports are also needed, such as those found in the Work and Family Bill of Rights (www.takecarenet.org). Universal health care, paid family and medical leave, a living wage, and quality, affordable child and elder care would go a long way toward closing the care gap. We are fortunate to live in a time when these issues are resonating both with voters and particularly with the leading Democratic contenders for the 2008 presidential elections. So the message here is twofold: if we are to close the care gap, we need to create more inclusive workplaces and communities *and* to press our elected officials and candidates to provide social supports.

Economist Robert Drago is professor of labor studies and women's studies at the Pennsylvania State University and a professorial fellow at the University of Melbourne. The author of four books and over 70 articles, his most recent book is Striking a Balance, *published by* Dollars & Sense *in 2007.*

SOURCES: Peter Brandon, "Determinants of Self-Care Arrangements among School-Aged Children," *Children and Youth Services Review*, 1999; Kristin Smith, "Who's Minding the Kids? Child Care Arrangements, Fall 1995," *Current Population Reports*, U.S. Census Bureau, 2000; Julie Meyer, *Age 2000: Census 2000 Brief*, U.S. Census Bureau, 2001; Heather Boushey et al., *Hardships in America: The Real Story of Working Families*, Economic Policy Institute, 2001; U.S. Dept. of Commerce, *National Estimates by Age, Sex, Race: 1900-1979 (PE-11)*, www.census.gov/popest/archives/pre-1980/PE-11.html; 2004 American Community Survey, U.S. Census Bureau, *American FactFinder* www.census.gov, Table S1801; CPS Annual Demographic Survey, U.S. Census Bureau, American FactFinder, www.census.gov, Table POV01; Janet C. Gornick and Marcia K. Meyers, *Families that Work: Policies for Reconciling Parenthood and Employment*, Russell Sage, 2003; Afterschool Alliance, "America After 3 PM: A Household Survey on Afterschool in America," 2004; Abt Associates, *Appropriateness of Minimum Nurse Staffing Ratios in Nursing Homes*, Phase II Final Report to the U.S. Department of Health and Human Services, 2001.

Article 6

THE 800-POUND RONALD MCDONALD IN THE ROOM

HELEN SCHARBER
February 2007

When your child's doctor gives you advice, you're probably inclined to take it. And if 60,000 doctors gave you advice, ignoring it would be even more difficult to justify. Last month, the American Academy of Pediatrics (AAP) issued a policy statement advising us to limit advertising to children, citing its adverse effects on health. Yes, banning toy commercials might result in fewer headaches for parents ("Please, please, pleeeeeeease, can I have this new video game I just saw 10 commercials for????"), but the AAP is more concerned with other health issues, such as childhood obesity. Advertising in general—and to children specifically—has reached astonishingly high levels, and as a country, we'd be wise to take the doctors' orders.

Advertising to kids is not a new phenomenon, but the intensity of it is. According to Juliet Schor, author of Born to Buy, companies spent around $100 million in 1983 on television advertising to kids. A little more than 20 years later, the amount earmarked for child-targeted ads in a variety of media has jumped to at least $12 billion annually. That's over $150 per boy and girl in the U.S. And it's not as though kids only see ads for action figures and sugary cereal; the other $240 billion spent on advertising each year ensures that they see ads for all kinds of products, everywhere they go. According to the AAP report, "the average young person views more than 3,000 ads per day on television, on the Internet, on billboards, and in magazines." Ads are also creeping into schools, where marketers have cleverly placed them in "educational" posters, textbook covers, bathroom stalls, scoreboards, daily news programs, and bus radio programming.

If advertising to children is becoming increasingly ubiquitous, it's probably because it's becoming increasingly profitable. Once upon a time, kids didn't have as much market power as they do today. The AAP report estimates that kids under 12 now spend $25 billion of their own money annually, teenagers spend another $155 billion, and both groups probably influence around $200 billion in parental spending. Not too surprising, considering that 62 percent of parents say their children "actively participate" in car-buying decisions, according to a study by J.D. Power & Associates (see the "Car makers direct more ads at kids" link below.) Marketers are also becoming more aware of the long-term potential of advertising to children. While they may not be the primary market now, they will be someday. And since researchers have found that kids as young as two can express preferences for specific brands, it's practically never too early to begin instilling brand loyalty.

But while small children have an incredible memory for commercial messages, they may not have developed the cognitive skills necessary to be critical of them. In 2004, the American Psychological Association (APA) also called for setting limits on advertising to kids, citing research that "children under the age of eight are unable to critically comprehend televised advertising messages and are prone to accept advertiser messages as truthful, accurate and unbiased." Many people take offense at the idea that we might be manipulated by marketing. Aren't we, after all, intelligent enough to make up our own minds about what to buy? The research cited by the APA, however, shows that children are uniquely vulnerable to manipulation by advertising. Marketers therefore should not be allowed to prey on them in the name of free speech.

Such invasive advertising to children is not only an ethical problem. The American Academy of Pediatrics cited advertising's effects on health through the promotion of unhealthy eating, drinking and smoking as the main motivation for setting limits. Children's health issues certainly merit attention. The Center for Disease Control, for example, has found that the prevalence of overweight children (ages 6 to 11) increased from 7 percent in 1980 to about 19 percent in 2004, while the rate among adolescents (ages 12 to 19) jumped from 5 percent to 17 percent. In addition to physical health problems, Schor argues that extensive marketing has negative effects on children's emotional well being. In her research for Born to Buy, Schor found links between immersion in consumer culture and depression, anxiety, low self esteem and conflicts with parents. The big push to consume can also lead to financial health problems, as many Americans know all too well, with credit card debt among 18- to 24-year-olds doubling over the past decade.

Not even the staunchest critics of marketing to children would argue that advertisements are completely at fault for these trends. Yet, the commercialization of nearly everything is negatively affecting children's well being in rather profound ways. Why, then, is hardly anyone paying attention to the 800-pound Ronald McDonald in the room? Perhaps it's because advertising appears to be a necessary evil or a fair tradeoff – maybe little Emma's school couldn't afford a soccer team without Coke on the scoreboard, for example. Or perhaps some would argue that parents who don't approve of the commercial culture should limit their kids' exposure to it. (See the Kids and Commercialism link below for tips on parenting kids in a commercial culture.) Increasingly invasive marketing techniques make it practically impossible to simply opt out of commercial culture, though. Thus, decisions to limit marketing to children must be made by the country as a whole. Sweden, Norway, Greece, Denmark, and Belgium have already passed laws curbing kid-targeted advertising, and according to 60,000 pediatricians, if we care about the health of our kids, we should too.

Helen Scharber is a staff economist for the Center for Popular Economics.

RESOURCES: American Association of Pediatrics, Policy Statement on Children, Adolescents, and Advertising, December 2006 (pediatrics.aappublications.org/cgi/content/full/118/6/2563); American Psychological Association, "Television Advertising Leads to Unhealthy Habits in Childen" February 2004; Jennifer Saranow, "Car makers direct more ads at kids," *Wall Street Journal*, November 9th, 2006; David Burke, "Two-year olds branded by TV advertising" (www.whitedot.org/issue/iss_story.asp?slug=Valkenburg); Center for a New American Dream, *Kids and Commercialism* (www.newdream.org/kids/); Juliet Schor, Born to Buy: The Commercialized Child and the New Consumer Culture (New York: Scribner, 2004); Center for Disease Control, "Facts about Childhood Overweight" (www.cdc.gov/HealthyYouth/overweight/index.htm).

Article 7

THE OPPOSITE OF INSURANCE
Unless you're rich, healthy, or both, Health Savings Accounts are bad news.

JAMES WOOLMAN
November/December 2006

Congress created Health Savings Accounts (HSAs) in 2003 as tax-advantaged savings accounts linked to the purchase of a high-deductible health plan. But the scheme is not a new idea. HSA proponents, including many health economists, have long argued that standard "comprehensive" insurance policies are too generous, sheltering consumers from the true cost of medical care. "Empowering" consumers to decide for themselves how much money to save for medical expenses, the theory goes, will unleash the magic of the market; costs will decline and quality will improve as doctors, hospitals, and other providers compete for discriminating customers.

New research on consumer and employer experiences with HSAs, however, confirms many of the fears cited by critics of the plans. The evidence shows that these plans attract relatively high-income, healthy people who are attracted to the tax benefits, while they place other consumers—including those with families, health problems, or low incomes—at risk for steep increases in out-of-pocket spending.

The Mechanics of HSAs

Workers can contribute pre-tax income to an HSA and can withdraw from it at any time for health-related spending. Employers may also contribute to employees' HSAs. Any money remaining at the end of the year stays in the account, enjoys tax benefits, and can be invested just like money in an Individual Retirement Account.

To open an HSA, however, you must have a high-deductible health insurance plan, and you *cannot* have ordinary health coverage. To qualify, a plan must have a deductible of at least $1,050 for an individual or $2,100 for a family. (HSA-qualified plans are allowed to cover some preventive care without a deductible.) Actual deductibles are much higher: in 2006 HSA-qualified plans had average deductibles of around $2,000 (individual) or $4,000 (family). Under the HSA scheme, in other words, a family typically has to pay the first $4,000 in medical bills each year out of pocket; their insurance plan kicks in—with all of the usual co-pays, exclusions, etc.—only after annual medical expenses exceed that amount.

The funds in the HSA are supposed to cover a portion of these out-of-pocket expenses, but workers are wholly responsible for any gap between the amount in their HSA and the amount of the deductible. The gap can be sizeable. A national survey by the Kaiser Family Foundation found the average deductible for a family HSA plan was $4,008, while the average employer HSA contribution was $1,139. Enrollees are fully responsible for the $2,869 gap, in addition to their premium payments and additional co-pays (see Figure 1).

By reducing employers' premium costs, limiting the amount of services employees are likely to use, and increasing the likelihood that employees will pay more out of pocket for health care, high-deductible plans shift financial risk from employers onto employees. Monthly premiums are lower under these plans than for comprehensive insurance, but high-deductible plan enrollees are still much more likely to spend a substantial amount of their income on health expenses than people enrolled in comprehensive plans. For instance, 31% of enrollees in HSA-type plans spent over 5% of their income on medical expenses, including premiums, compared with only 12% of enrollees in comprehensive plans, according to a recent survey conducted by the Employee Benefits Research Institute and the Commonwealth Fund (see Figure 2).

Flawed Plan

Proponents of HSAs would say this shifting of risk is a good thing: a market-based reform to address escalating health care costs. But this is a deeply flawed view.

For one thing, high-deductible plans are unlikely to have much impact on overall health care spending, most of which results from expensive treatments for serious illnesses whose costs exceed the high deductibles. One recent study found that more than 95% of medical expenditures by working-age households with health

---

FIGURE 1

THE HEALTH SAVINGS ACCOUNT/HIGH DEDUCTIBLE HEALTH PLAN SCHEME: WORKERS PAY MORE, EMPLOYERS PAY LESS

Annual Worker Contribution Comparison

	Single All Plans	Single HDHP	Family All Plans	Family HDHP
Worker Premium Contribution	$624	$467	$2,976	$2,115
Deductible	$508	$2,011	$1,099	$4,008
Employer HSA Contribution		($988)		($1,139)
Total Potential Out-of-Pocket*	$1,132	$1,490	$4,075	$4,984

Annual Employer Contribution Comparison

	Single All Plans	Single HDHP	Family All Plans	Family HDHP
Employer Premium Contribution	$4,248	$2,709	$7,756	$6,400
Employer HSA Contribution		$988		$1,139
Total Employer Spending	$4,248	$3,697	$7,756	$7,539

* Totals do not include coinsurance.

Source: The Kaiser Family Foundation and The Health Research and Education Trust 2006 Employer Benefits Survey.

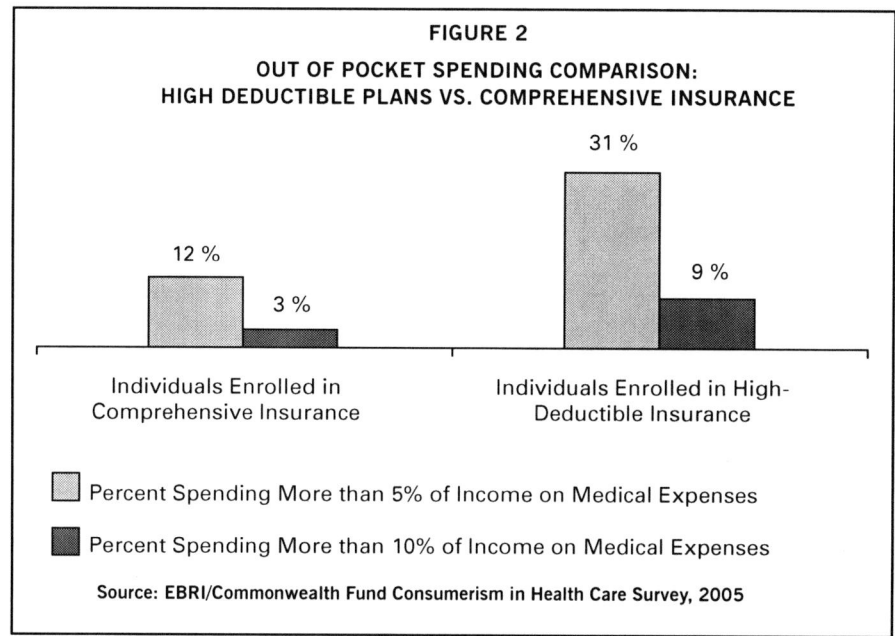

insurance were made by those who spend above the minimum HSA deductibles, and that overall, nearly 79% of total medical expenditures occurred above the minimum HSA deductibles. In fact, the only type of spending HSAs are likely to reduce is the kind we want to encourage: primary and preventive care. According to the Commonwealth Fund, enrollees with deductibles over $1,000 were twice as likely as enrollees with deductibles under $500 to avoid seeing the doctor for a medical problem, avoid seeing a specialist, or skip a recommended treatment due to cost.

Moreover, people do not and cannot shop for health care services as they do for other goods. Most people do not have adequate information on the cost and quality of care to make informed purchasing decisions. Nor are they inclined to do so when they are sick or in distress, which is when health care decisions are typically made. Most people enrolled in high-deductible plans do not, in fact, shop for less expensive care, although many shop for better prescription drug prices, according to a 2006 Government Accountability Office (GAO) report.

The GAO found that current HSA participants are disproportionately high-income, healthy people who will benefit from the tax advantages and are unlikely to need much health care. Although generally satisfied with their own experience, HSA enrollees polled by the GAO said they would *not* recommend high-deductible plans for people with families, health problems, maintenance medications, or moderate incomes—in other words, most people.

So HSAs represent a double-edged sword. If large numbers of people are forced to switch from comprehensive health coverage to high-deductible plans, they will likely face significantly higher out-of-pocket costs. On the other hand, if HSAs continue to attract the healthiest enrollees, the exit of this healthy segment from the comprehensive coverage pool will likely drive up health insurance costs for everyone else.

HSAs and high-deductible plans appeal to employers looking to cut health care costs, high-income earners looking for more tax breaks, and younger workers willing to gamble they won't get sick. For most people, however, they are the opposite of insurance: they concentrate the financial risk of illness instead of spreading it, and they increase the likelihood of incurring medical debt instead of reducing it.

James Woolman is a health policy analyst and a member of the D&S *collective.*

SOURCES: "Consumer-Directed Health Plans: Early Enrollee Experiences with Health Savings Accounts and Eligible Health Plans," GAO, 8/06; Kaiser Family Foundation and Health Research and Educational Trust, "Employer Health Benefits: 2006 Annual Survey," 9/06; Paul Fronstin and Sara R. Collins, "Early Experience With High-Deductible and Consumer-Driven Health Plans," Employee Benefits Research Institute and the Commonwealth Fund, 12/05; Edwin Park and Robert Greenstein, "Latest Enrollment Data Still Fail to Dispel Concerns about Health Savings Accounts," Center on Budget and Policy Priorities, 1/30/06.

Article 8

MEDICAID AND MEDICARE CUTS
(Almost) Everyone Pays

SAM URETSKY
July/August 2006

Unless you belong to the select and dwindling group of those with fully employer-paid health coverage—or to the 40-million-and-counting with no health insurance at all—you've probably noticed your health insurance premiums rising at a frightening pace. In 2005, premiums for family coverage rose by an average of 9.2%, six percentage points more than the rate of inflation, according to the Kaiser Family Foundation's *Annual Survey Of Employer Health Benefits*. The cost of health insurance has increased by 73% since 2000, with an average family plan costing $10,880 in 2005; the average monthly premium contribution paid by employees with family plans rose from $135 in 2000 to $226 in 2005.

There is plenty of blame to go around for rising health insurance costs. But an under-recognized part of the story lies in the shifting of costs from public to private insurers. This May, Premera Blue Cross, a Washington state insurer, released a study of public versus private reimbursements to hospitals and doctors. The study found that "employers and consumers are paying billions of dollars more a year for medical care to compensate for imbalances in the nation's health care system resulting from tight Medicare and Medicaid budgets" and pointed to "a rapid acceleration in higher costs to private payers in Washington state, for example, as hospitals and doctors grapple with constraints in the federal health insurance programs," as the *New*

York Times summed it up.

The Premera study found that in 2004, Washington state hospitals had losses of 15.4% for services to Medicare beneficiaries, compared to *profits* of 2.9% for these services in 1997. Over the same period, hospitals' profit margins for patients with employer-sponsored health plans *rose*, from 5% to 16.4%. As the report put it, "This phenomenon can be thought of as a cost shift from the public programs to commercial payers. That is, if Medicare and Medicaid had paid higher hospital rates, commercial payer rates could have been lower with hospitals still achieving the same ... operating margins." The study found a similar trend for doctors' offices. Medicare pays physicians 25% to 31% less than private insurers do in Washington, and Medicaid pays about 30% less than private insurers for children's office visits and up to 54% less for adults' office visits.

In sum, the study found that hospitals in Washington state charged private insurers an additional $738 million in 2004 to compensate for losses incurred by treating patients under Medicare and Medicaid. Through the 1990s, by contrast, treatment of Medicare and Medicaid patients was profitable for both hospitals and physicians. The percentage profit was small—about 2% in Washington state—but it meant that Medicare and Medicaid were covering all direct expenses for their patients.

What accounts for this sharp reversal? The simple answer: the Bush tax cuts. In 2001, Bush inherited a 10-year budget surplus of around $5.6 trillion, according to Congressional Budget Office projections. "We can proceed with tax relief without fear of budget deficits, even if the economy softens. ... The projections for the surplus in my budget are cautious and conservative," the president claimed. But 2000 was the last year the United States ran a budget surplus. Between 2001 and 2003, the federal government saw that projected $5.6 trillion 10-year surplus turn into a projected 10-year deficit of $378 billion. And the 2001 and 2003 tax cuts, primarily benefiting the wealthiest families, were the single most important cause of the new deficits, according to analyses by the Congressional Budget Office and the Center on Budget and Policy Priorities, among others.

Between 2001 and 2005, Medicare and Medicaid spending per beneficiary did grow, but only very slightly—far less than the rise in health care costs. So the gap between how much hospitals and doctors were spending to provide care and how much they were being reimbursed under the two programs grew. And the situation is about to get even worse. To deal with the growing deficits, last year Congress passed the Deficit Reduction Act of 2005. The new law did nothing to restore earlier tax levels, but did make major cuts in Medicare and Medicaid funding. For instance, the law cuts Medicaid spending by $4.8 billion over the next five years and by $26.1 billion over the next 10 years. The direct effects of these cuts will be to reduce reimbursements to hospitals and physicians—more of the income shortfalls described in the Premera report. No doubt these shortfalls will result in more cost shifting onto those with private coverage, who will continue to face steep increases in their premiums.

Of course, Medicare and Medicaid recipients are hurt by the cuts too. Under the 2005 law, states will be allowed to tighten restrictions on Medicaid eligibility and impose higher co-payments for some drugs and services. The law cuts spending on acute care health services for children by 15% and on acute care for the elderly poor by 8%. Elderly people who require nursing home care will be less able to protect their assets, although 84% of nursing home residents have assets of less than a single year's nursing home costs.

So, tax cuts for the wealthy are paid for in part by cuts in services to the elderly and poor, and by making private health insurance costs even more burdensome for employees who have coverage and employers who provide it.

But there's one group not burdened at all by these difficulties: top health insurance executives. In 2003, the nonprofit watchdog group FamiliesUSA issued a report on executive pay in the 11 for-profit, publicly-traded health insurance companies that offer so-called Medicare+Choice plans, under which Medicare beneficiaries receive their coverage through a private insurer rather than directly from Medicare. Annual CEO compensation ranged from $1.6 million at Humana to $76 million at Oxford, with an average of $15.1 million. And these figures do not include the average of $57.6 million in unexercised stock options these top dogs held. Since executive pay is part of the overhead cost of running an insurance company, it's no wonder that traditional Medicare, which paid *its* chief executive $130,000 in 2002—and with no stock options—is able to operate with overhead costs of around 1%, while the private sector has overhead costs of 10% to 15%.

To the credit of Premera Blue Cross, which paid for the Washington state study on cost-shifting, in 1999 its CEO was paid a relatively modest $736,650. On the other hand, Premera has applied to change from a nonprofit to a for-profit corporation, in spite of opposition from consumer groups who believe a for-profit company will increase rates and reduce services.

Top insurance executives are among the super-high-income elite, and as such, prime beneficiaries of the Bush tax cuts. (Not to mention that their role in the design of Medicare's new prescription drug benefit, which cuts private insurers in on the program, is also contributing to the budget deficit.) When the federal government tried to make up the revenue lost to tax cuts by cutting benefits and reimbursements under Medicare and Medicaid, these same insurance companies cried foul. It is good to see CEOs advocating for increased funding of social programs. Now maybe they could offer to give back part of their tax-cut bonus to help pay the bill.

Sam Uretsky is a retired hospital pharmacist who frequently writes about health care policy and financing.

SOURCES: Milt Freudenheim, "Low Payments by U.S. Raise Medical Bills Billions a Year," *New York Times*, 6/1/06; Premera Blue Cross, "Payment Level Comparison between Public Programs and Commercial Health Plans for Washington State Hospitals and Physicians," (Milliman Consultants & Actuaries, May 2006); Families USA, "Top Dollar: CEO Compensation in Medicare's Private Insurance Plans," June 2003; John Holahan and Mindy Cohen, "Understanding the Recent Changes in Medicaid Spending and Enrollment Growth," (Kaiser Commission on Medicaid and the Uninsured, May 2006).

Article 9

KATRINA HITS CANCER ALLEY
An Interview with Environmental Justice Activist Monique Harden.

March/April 2006

The environmental, economic justice, and antiracism movements have not always been on the same page. A growing number of activists in all three, however, have begun to recognize that comprehensive analyses and strategies that address ecological devastation and economic and racial injustice together are indispensable. No one better embodies that crucial advance than Monique Harden. Harden is codirector of Advocates for Environmental Human Rights, a nonprofit, public interest law firm in New Orleans that she cofounded with attorney Nathalie Walker in 2002. Harden also coordinates international coalitions of community organizations advocating for human rights and environmental justice. Here are excerpts from D&S collective member Ben Greenberg's interview with Harden in New Orleans this January. —Eds.

BEN GREENBERG: Let's start with the immediate environmental impacts of Katrina. What kinds of hazardous substances did the storm release?

MONIQUE HARDEN: It's important to understand the significant number of industrial facilities operating in Louisiana and the massive amount of toxic pollution that these industries release into our air, water, and land. Between New Orleans and Baton Rouge, an area known as "Cancer Alley," there are approximately 130 oil refineries and petrochemical facilities. When you are aware of the industrial pollution all around us, you can understand the toxic impact of forceful hurricane winds pushing onto communities the water and sediment that have received industrial discharges for many decades.

Our organization, Advocates for Environmental Human Rights, has been working with several groups to take samples of the sediment left behind after the flood waters were drained. We didn't want a replay of what EPA did in New York after 9/11—claiming that air quality was good when in fact it was very unhealthy. So, early on, Wilma Subra, a chemist in Louisiana, began taking sediment samples and analyzing them for our organizations. Both her sampling analysis and the tests that EPA conducted revealed high levels of contaminants in the sediment covering yards, streets, and sidewalks in flooded communities. Arsenic and diesel fuel substances are the most prevalent but not the only contaminants. However, EPA concluded that only more retesting and analysis was needed. We saw it very differently and have been demanding that the agency take action to immediately clean up the sediment.

The problem here is that EPA has not established a standard for cleaning up toxic sediment or soil; instead the agency has only established standards for further assessment. But we have looked at various Superfund sites and found that EPA has set, on a case-by-case basis, requirements for cleaning up these sites that should, at the very least, apply to our Gulf Coast communities. For example, in the PAB Oil &

Chemical Services site in Louisiana, EPA required that arsenic in the soil be cleaned up so that no more than 10 milligrams per kilogram of arsenic remains in the soil on this site. In neighborhoods that were flooded in New Orleans, there are sediment-arsenic concentrations that are over 70 milligrams per kilogram. EPA's inaction threatens the health of residents who have returned to communities with contaminated sediment. Children, the elderly, and other people with poor health are particularly vulnerable to the toxins that EPA refuses to clean up.

After Hurricane Katrina, federal and state health agencies posted notices advising people to wear protective gear, such as Tyvek suits, respirator masks, gloves, and shoe covers, but not one government agency provides this protective gear to people returning to the area. Instead, a few nonprofit organizations have raised funds to deliver protective gear and health information to people. But these efforts are a drop in the bucket. For example, on December 1st, when a section of the Lower Ninth Ward was opened to residents, our organizations ran out of Tyvek suits—we had 1,000—and all the other protective gear in the first two and a half hours. Many more people needed this protective gear, but we couldn't help them. I felt terrible that our help was not enough and that our government could care less about protecting our health. In response to our requests, the city of New Orleans submitted an application to FEMA for protective gear, but there has been no response.

BG: Tell me about the work that Advocates for Environmental Human Rights was doing before Katrina.

MH: Our mission is to advance and defend the human right to a healthy environment. We provide litigation, public advocacy, and community organizing support—all with the aim of reforming severe flaws in the U.S. environmental regulatory system that allow fundamental human rights to life, health, and racial equality to be violated. The failure of EPA to clean up contaminated sediment in Gulf Coast communities is part of a systemic problem; it underscores just how irrelevant human health protection is to the environmental regulatory system, notwithstanding the volumes of environmental laws and regulations established by our government.

BG: So your approach is to work on local issues but affect national policy?

MH: That's correct. In March 2005, AEHR filed the first-ever human rights legal challenge against the United States for its failed environmental regulatory system. We prepared that litigation on behalf of Mossville, a historic African-American community in the southwest corner of Louisiana. In this petition, we sought specific health and environmental remedies for Mossville residents, as well as reform of the U.S. environmental regulatory system. We filed the petition with the Inter-American Commission on Human Rights of the Organization of American States.

BG: What company or companies were in violation of those residents' human rights and what were the specific environmental problems?

MH: First of all, let me clarify: we are not charging the companies; we are charging the U.S. government for violating the human rights of Mossville residents. The government has authorized corporations that own fourteen toxic facilities in and around Mossville to endanger the lives of Mossville residents, harm their health, and burden this African-American community with millions of pounds of toxic chemicals that have made the air unhealthy, poisoned fish in local waters, and contaminated the soil.

What's more, a federal agency, the Agency for Toxic Substances and Disease Registry, has conducted dioxin testing of Mossville residents' blood, showing average dioxin concentrations that are three times higher than the national average. Dioxin can cause cancer and other serious health problems. However, this agency has resisted assisting the community in its demands for medical monitoring and health care.

Notwithstanding years of work by Mossville Environmental Action Now, our federal and state environmental and health agencies have not taken any meaningful action that protects the health of people living in Mossville. Instead these agencies issue more and more permits that allow the industrial facilities to increase pollution.

Demanding human rights protection is critical to ending this injustice, which is why Mossville Environmental Action Now and AEHR filed the legal petition with the Inter-American Commission on Human Rights. This commission, like so many other human rights judicial bodies, has determined that a government's failure to adequately protect the environment can violate human rights. In Mossville, and many other people of color and poor communities, fundamental human rights to life, health, and racial equality are trampled on by the U.S. system of so-called "environmental protection."

BG: Can you give a little background on Mossville?

MH: Mossville was founded in the 1790s by emancipated Blacks. It was a place where people could go and raise their families in a safe haven from the racial hostility that was all around them. There's some history written on Mossville—elder Mossville residents will tell you that in the past the community was able to thrive because of its rich natural resources. Folks were able to farm, hunt, and fish; businesses were able to develop from those natural resources.

However, Mossville was never incorporated and did not have governance authority. Zoning and other decisions were made by the parish [county], state, and federal governments. Remember, when industrial facilities were getting their foothold in Mossville and other parts of Louisiana, the 1930s through the 1950s, African Americans in the South did not have the right to vote and were oppressed and discriminated against by Jim Crow laws. So when industrial facilities began popping up in Louisiana, Mossville residents had no say in where they would locate, and this became an area that was targeted for industrial development. People in Mossville were not able to challenge, much less resist, the industrialization of their community.

Today, in and around Mossville, there are an oil refinery complex owned by Conoco Phillips, a coal-fired power plant owned by Entergy, five vinyl production facilities—the largest of which are PPG Industries and Georgia Gulf—and six other petrochemical facilities. All of these facilities are operating and spewing pollution within a quarter-mile of the community. Several have reported that Mossville residents would be killed if there was a catastrophic leak of chlorine gas or an explosion of petroleum-based products. You would think that with such hazards these facilities would operate safely, but they have frequent industrial accidents.

BG: How large a community is Mossville?

MH: It's a community of approximately 1,000 residents.

BG: Listening to you speak about Mossville, it's staggering to understand just how directly the situation there is the outgrowth of U.S. racism. It's a very direct relationship.

MH: Absolutely, and Mossville shares many commonalities with other communities—whether the residents are African American, Latino, Asian American, Native American, or poor whites. When you're dealing with environmental justice there are very strong historical ties to political and economic systems that have marginalized and exploited people of color and the poor.

BG: Can you talk about how economic policies have contributed to environmental racism in Louisiana?

MH: Sure. You have to understand that Louisiana has only known two forms of economic development: slave plantations and heavy industry. In fact, many of the industrial facilities are located on former slave plantations, and a few companies have applied the names of these plantations to their facilities. It's no accident that many of these facilities are located in close proximity to communities with mostly African-American residents.

Seventy years or so after the Civil War, investment in industrial manufacturing began to pick up in the state because of its natural resources, especially oil and navigable waters. The state government lured companies by enacting a statewide tax exemption in 1936. Under the Industrial Property Tax Exemption, as it's called, new facilities are exempt from paying property taxes on their facilities for up to 10 years. Then, if a company puts new capital investment into an existing facility, its exemption is renewed; this can go on into perpetuity.

The problem with the industrial tax exemption, of course, is that it has become a form of corporate welfare for companies like Exxon and Shell that are now wealthier than many countries. The largesse that these companies have acquired has also made them politically powerful in the legislature and allowed them to run roughshod over environmental and worker-safety laws. So, we now have aging and accident-prone industrial facilities largely dumping pollution in African-American communities like Mossville. And a prevailing political and economic climate in Louisiana and the United States in which these industrial corporations set the agenda.

One result is poverty. Dr. Paul Templet, a professor at Louisiana State University, has correlated pollution and poverty. In a nutshell, his research shows that the more industrial pollution a state has, the more poverty that state has. In Louisiana, we have one of the highest rates both of poverty and of industrial pollution. His analysis shows that stricter environmental standards that reduce industrial pollution require more jobs, which means more economic investment in the state and in the people in the state. A thriving economy requires good environmental conditions.

BG: Can you talk about where Katrina fits in?

MH: Katrina hit a state that has encouraged oil companies to install a broad network of oil pipelines that have destroyed coastal wetlands. If they were still intact, these wetlands would have absorbed some of the hurricane's force and reduced its damage. At the same time, our state embraces industries whose increasing emissions contribute to the global warming effect of hurricanes becoming more intense. And our state has provided these companies with a man-made canal—the Mississippi River Gulf Outlet—that not only damaged wetlands, but actually served to funnel Katrina's storm surge into our communities in St. Bernard and Orleans parishes.

BG: New Orleans obviously faces a crisis now in terms of rebuilding a viable economy. What are the roles of these companies in creating the new economic life of the area?

MH: I want to be clear that before Hurricane Katrina, neither New Orleans nor the state of Louisiana had what could be called a viable economy. Basic things like public school education and health care have been underfunded for years. It's now a struggle for all of us just to get back to having poor and inadequate public school and health care systems.

Instead of figuring out how we can do it better, much of the focus has been on planning ways to keep poor and mostly African-American people out of the state. The people who suffered the most from the failed levee systems and outrageous governmental neglect in the days following Katrina are now being targeted with governmental plans and actions that block their return home. I guess the thinking is that if you lock out poor people, the economy will improve.

Millions of our taxpayer dollars have gone to restoring oil company pipelines and other infrastructure that has devastated our environment and made us more vulnerable to hurricanes. In contrast, hurricane-damaged communities have not been restored. Another glimpse into how oil companies and the economy may intersect after Katrina is the announcement that Shell will cosponsor, for the first time, the New Orleans Jazz Fest. The company has been lauded as a savior of this cultural event; this view completely ignores how Shell has contributed to the disastrous consequences of Hurricane Katrina.

BG: Could you give a breakdown of some of the specific communities in New Orleans and the environmental problems they face?

MH: Gert Town is an African-American neighborhood in New Orleans where the Thompson Hayward Company mixed pesticides, herbicides, and dry cleaning agents across the street from residents' homes and churches for approximately 40 years. This plant was shut down in the 1980s when it was discovered to be illegally dumping chemicals into the city's drainage system. That triggered enforcement that amounted to nothing more than a "cooperative agreement" between the state Department of Environmental Quality (DEQ) and the company owners for cleaning up waste contaminated with DDT and other banned chemicals. The agreement set out a series of cleanup steps and a schedule of 90 days or less for each step. However, nearly 20 years later, four million pounds of contaminated waste have yet to be removed.

Days before Hurricane Katrina struck, the community, organized as Gert Town Revival Initiative, and AEHR had compelled DEQ to allow the community to participate in the design of the cleanup plan. Then the hurricane came, causing four feet of flooding in Gert Town. Sediment sampling now shows the presence of DDT and other chemicals from Thompson Hayward, in addition to the arsenic and diesel fuel substances. This means that the storm moved pesticides and other chemicals from the site into the community.

BG: And there are other communities with similar problems?

MH: Yes. There's the Agriculture Street community. This subdivision was built in the 1960s and 1970s and marketed to African Americans. People who bought these houses or moved into the rental units had no idea their homes were built on top of a toxic landfill. It was only after residents began to realize that they and their neighbors suffered serious health problems, including cancer, that they learned about the toxic landfill underneath them. A study by a state agency showed that Agriculture Street residents had the highest incidence of breast cancer statewide for both women and men.

In 1994 the community was designated a Superfund site. EPA provided a ridiculous cleanup that involved removing one to two feet of contaminated soil from yards that have 17 feet of soil contaminated with over 150 toxic chemicals and heavy metals. And EPA refused to temporarily relocate residents who were exposed to toxins during over a year of excavation.

Residents have had to sue federal and state housing agencies and other responsible government agencies for building their subdivision on top a toxic landfill. A few weeks ago, residents won their lawsuit in a state court, but the government defendants are expected to appeal.

BG: How has the situation been compounded since Katrina?

MH: People have no homes! During Katrina, the failure of the levees flooded this neighborhood with water as high as nine feet. Homes are covered in toxic mold and many have extensive structural damage. Many of the hazardous contaminants that triggered EPA's Superfund site designation and were supposed to be trapped underground are now present in the sediment. Residents are wrestling with insurance companies and mortgage companies. Some have been able to secure homes elsewhere, but not others.

BG: What are some of the challenges facing New Orleans residents who want to return home to environmentally safe neighborhoods?

MH: Sediment contamination is a representative problem. EPA is not cleaning up the sediment because reconstruction money is being spent on everything *except for* enabling people to return and rebuild their communities. Federal spending on Hurricane Katrina is a boondoggle for contractors and government agencies. For example, $3 million of hurricane relief spending went to the Department of Defense for the purchase of ammunition. This is outrageous! Meanwhile, six months after Katrina, we still have communities that look like the hurricane passed yesterday.

In October 2004, the federal government instituted the so-called "Assistance to Internally Displaced Persons Policy," which states what our government is committed to do in order to protect the human rights of people displaced from their communities by natural disasters. This policy commits our government to providing comprehensive assistance, from immediate disaster response through long-term development support. Even though this policy was developed by the U.S. Agency for International Development and, presumably, directed to internally displaced persons in foreign countries, we believe that our government should, at a minimum, exercise the same care and commitment to protecting the human rights of people in our country who are still in need of the humanitarian assistance, the return and transition assistance, and the long-term development assistance that are articulated in this policy.

BG: A lot of the organizing in New Orleans now involves local groups allied with national ones. Can you talk about the role of people and nonprofits outside of New Orleans?

MH: Post-Hurricane Katrina, there are national and local organizations that are doing a great job of working together for justice. There are also groups that are exploiting Hurricane Katrina for their own benefit. People who couldn't find the Ninth Ward or Chalmette on a map are now working in the position of "Katrina Policy Chief"—I'm not making this up, it's an actual position—in organizations that have no relationship with local communities.

In my organizing experience, the formula for success is working in service of communities that are directly harmed by injustice. The formula for failure is creating coalitions that do not respect the need for communities to be organized and self-determined. Social transformation can only be achieved through community organizing. Without organized communities speaking for themselves and guiding the work of coalitions, you just have a bunch of groups trying to feel important.

BG: Last September you said on the radio show "Living On Earth" that you were optimistic, that "this is an opportunity for us to transform in a progressive and positive way the lives of people in New Orleans and along the Gulf Coast of the United States." Five months later, are you still feeling optimistic?

MH: I'll go to my grave feeling optimistic about achieving social justice. And I say that because I know that the seed for achieving a just world is community organizing, and I know from experience that when communities are organized there's nothing that they can't achieve.

Article 10

MEDICARE PART D GETS AN "F"

JAMES WOOLMAN AND JAMES McBRIDE
January/February 2006

Medicare Part D, the new drug benefit package that went into effect at the beginning of 2006, is projected to cost $724 billion over 10 years. Not only is it expensive, it's confusing, and it provides more benefits to insurance companies than to enrollees. Here are five key reasons Medicare Part D deserves an "F":

1. Meager Benefits

Despite the program's huge cost, the actual benefits are minimal. A standard plan requires members to pay a $32 monthly premium, a $250 deductible, and 25% of drug costs up to $2,250. After that, they must pay 100% of the costs until their total drug spending reaches $5,100, then 5% of costs exceeding $5,100. Subsidies are available for low-income enrollees (those whose incomes are under 150% of the federal poverty line), but most participants will still have to pay the majority of their drug costs out of pocket (see Figure 1).

In addition, analysts predict one in four enrollees will actually end up spending *more* under the new plan than they would have without it. This is because many seniors who already have prescription drug coverage—through an employer, a supplemental Medicare policy, or Medicaid —will lose this coverage and be forced to accept the less generous benefits provided by Part D.

To make matters worse, the new drug plan may undermine one important source of prescription drugs for hundreds of thousands of people without health insurance: the pharmaceutical companies' patient assistance programs for the indigent. Some companies have said that anyone who signs up for Medicare D will become ineligible for such programs; others have indicated they will drop anyone who is even eligible for the new benefit.

2. Less Negotiating Power

Because conservatives have decreed that markets will always provide the lowest prices and the greatest efficiency, the new Medicare drug law explicitly bans the government from negotiating with drug companies. Of course, the federal government already negotiates directly with drug makers and receives deep discounts for drugs purchased by the Department of Defense and the Veterans Administration. According to a study done by the staff of Rep. Henry Waxman (D-Calif.), the price of a month's supply of the top ten drugs under Medicare D is 80% higher than the negotiated price the VA pays for those same drugs (see Figure 2). Rather than using the government's purchasing power to provide seniors with a better benefit, Congress, citing fears of "price controls," has essentially cut a blank check to the drug industry.

3. Less Consumer Protection

Enrollees who sign up after the May 15, 2006, deadline will incur a 1% per month penalty for every month they delay enrollment, with no limitation. For example, someone who signs up three years after the deadline will be charged an additional 36% on their premium, *forever*. This is designed to prevent people from signing up only when they know they will need expensive medications.

Once enrolled, consumers cannot change plans for a year. Insurance companies, however, are free to drop drugs from their coverage lists at any time, as long as they cover two drugs within each class of drugs used to treat similar conditions—for example, two statin drugs for high cholesterol. Consumers are stuck, even if their medical needs or the drugs offered by their plan change. There is an appeal process, but the law gives plans the power to decide whether or not to grant exceptions—and even allows them to overrule a patient's doctor.

4. Intoxication with Markets

Conservatives have been dying to privatize Medicare for years, and they got their way with Part D. Instead of being handled directly through Medicare, the prescription drug benefit will be delivered by private insurance companies through competing Prescription Drug Plans. The justification is that competitive markets will cut out government inefficiency and lower prices for consumers. (This justification is questionable from the start, of course, given that traditional Medicare, a government-run, single-payer system, has a super-low overhead of less than 4% *and* a high level of beneficiary satisfaction.)

However, unless insurance companies can screen patients or set higher prices for sicker people, they are reluctant to enter the market for providing drug insurance. So Congress packed the law with sweeteners to reduce the risk borne by companies. During the first two years, the government will pay 50% of the losses for plans whose costs are more than 2.5% higher than expected, and will also pay 80% of the costs of very expensive patients through a "reinsurance" provision. Insurers quickly realized that these terms make it nearly impossible to lose money, so many more than expected have chosen to participate.

The huge number of plans worsens another problem with the insurance market: consumer confusion.

FIGURE 1
2006 OUT-OF-POCKET SPENDING WITH STANDARD PART D BENEFIT PACKAGE

Annual Drug Costs	Out of Pocket Spending (Including Premiums)	Percent of Drug Costs Paid By Enrollee
$500	$699	140%
$1,000	$824	82%
$2,250	$1,136	51%
$3,000	$1,886	63%
$4,000	$2,886	72%
$5,100	$3,986	78%
$6,000	$4,031	67%
$8,000	$4,131	52%
$10,000	$4,231	42%

Spending calculations were based on the standard Part D benefit package.

Source for percent of enrollees: Actuarial Research Corp. and the Kaiser Family Foundation, Estimates of Medicare Beneficiaries Out-of-Pocket Drug Spending in 2006, November 2004.

With so many competing offers, it's hard for seniors to tell which plan is right for them. In many regions more than 40 plans are available, each with its own benefit and pricing structure. With limited time to choose, and with the financial and medical stakes high, seniors understandably feel overwhelmed. Republicans refer to this as "empowering the consumer." The rest of us call it stress.

5. Undermining Social Insurance

Part D is part of a larger effort to transform the health care system through market-based "reforms." These strategies, which include health savings accounts, high-deductible health plans, and tax credits for the purchase of individual insurance, are designed to reduce health spending by placing more financial burden on patients.

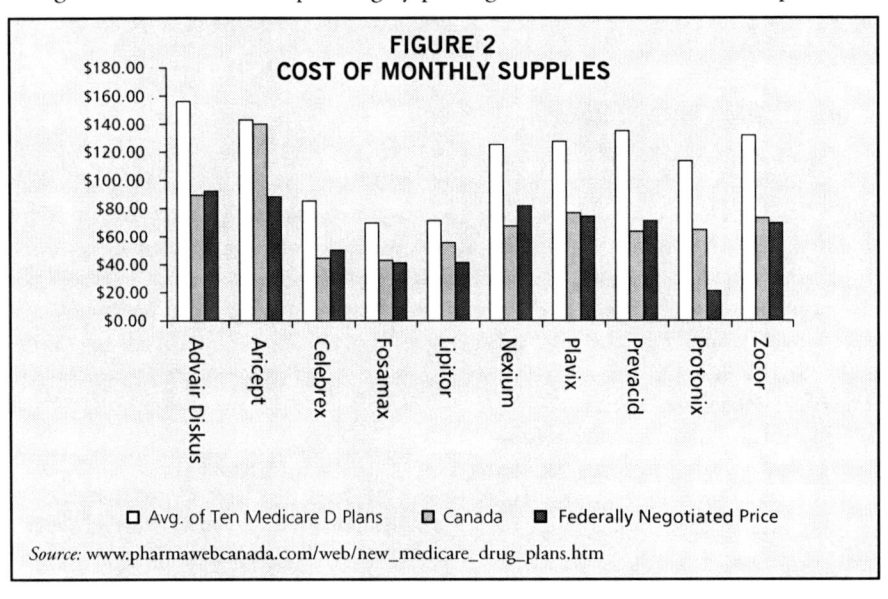

**FIGURE 2
COST OF MONTHLY SUPPLIES**

Bar chart comparing Avg. of Ten Medicare D Plans, Canada, and Federally Negotiated Price for: Advair Diskus, Aricept, Celebrex, Fosamax, Lipitor, Nexium, Plavix, Prevacid, Protonix, Zocor.

Source: www.pharmawebcanada.com/web/new_medicare_drug_plans.htm

A public plan, like the enormously popular traditional Medicare program, would have provided more benefit to more people at lower cost, and would not have required any of the backwards market fixes that make the Part D program so complex. In reality, private markets for individual health insurance do not work well—except for enriching corporations—and relying more heavily upon them will only further impoverish and destabilize our health care system.

James Woolman is a health policy analyst and a member of the D&S *collective.*

SOURCES: Geraldine Dalleck, "Consumer Protection Issues Raised by the Medicare Prescription Drug, Improvement, and Modernization Act of 2003," July 2004; Kaiser Family Foundation, "The Medicare Prescription Drug Benefit," September 2005; Actuarial Research Corp. and Kaiser Family Foundation, "Estimates of Medicare Beneficiaries Out-of-Pocket Drug Spending in 2006, Modeling the Impact of the MMA," November 2004, all available at www.kff.org/medicare/upload/; "Falling Short: Medicare Prescription Drug Plans Offer Meager Savings," Families USA

Special Report, December 2005; "Health Plans Undaunted By Medicare Part D," *Managed Care*, May 2005; "New Medicare Plan to Cut Off Free Drugs," *Philadelphia Inquirer*, 11/17/05.

Article 11

WHAT'S GOOD FOR WAL-MART ...

JOHN MILLER
January/February 2006

> "Is Wal-Mart Good for America?"
> It is a testament to the public relations of the anti-Wal-Mart campaign that the question above is even being asked.
>
> By any normal measure, Wal-Mart's business ought to be noncontroversial. It sells at low costs, albeit in mind-boggling quantities....
>
> The company's success and size ... do not rest on monopoly profits or price-gouging behavior. It simply sells things people will buy at small markups and, as in the old saw, makes it up on volume.... You may believe, as do service-workers unions and a clutch of coastal elites—many of whom, we'd wager, have never set foot in Wal-Mart—that Wal-Mart "exploits" workers who can't say no to low wages and poor benefits. You might accept the canard that it drives good local businesses into the ground, although both of these allegations are more myth than reality.
>
> But even if you buy into the myths, there's no getting around the fact that somewhere out there, millions of people are spending billions of dollars on what Wal-Mart puts on its shelves. No one is making them do it.... Wal-Mart can't make mom and pop shut down the shop anymore than it can make customers walk through the doors or pull out their wallets.
>
> What about the workers? ... Wal-Mart's average starting wage is already nearly double the national minimum of $5.15 an hour. The company has also recently increased its health-care for employees on the bottom rungs of the corporate ladder.
>
> —*Wall Street Journal* editorial, December 3, 2005

W ho's Number One? The Customer! Always!" The last line of Wal-Mart's company cheer just about sums up the *Wall Street Journal* editors' benign view of the behemoth corporation. But a more honest answer would be Wal-Mart itself: not the customer, and surely not the worker.

The first retail corporation to top the Fortune 500, Wal-Mart trailed only Exxon-Mobil in total revenues last year. With 1.6 million workers, 1.3 million in the United States and 300,000 offshore, Wal-Mart is the largest private employer in the nation and the world's largest retailer.

Being number one has paid off handsomely for the family of Wal-Mart founder Sam Walton. The family's combined fortune is now an estimated $90 billion, equal to the net worth of Bill Gates and Warren Buffett combined.

But is what's good for the Walton family good for America? Should we believe the editors that Wal-Mart's unprecedented size and market power have redounded not only to the Walton family's benefit but to ours as well?

Low Wages and Meager Benefits

Working for the world's largest employer sure hasn't paid off for Wal-Mart's employees. True, they have a job, and others without jobs line up to apply for theirs. But that says more about the sad state of today's labor market than the quality of Wal-Mart jobs. After all, less than half of Wal-Mart workers last a year, and turnover at the company is twice that at comparable retailers.

Why? Wal-Mart's oppressive working conditions surely have something to do with it. Wal-Mart has admitted to using minors to operate hazardous machinery, has been sued in six states for forcing employees to work off the books (i.e., unpaid) and without breaks, and is currently facing a suit brought by 1.6 million current and former female employees accusing Wal-Mart of gender discrimination. At the same time, Wal-Mart workers are paid less and receive fewer benefits than other retail workers.

Wal-Mart, according to its own reports, pays an average of $9.68 an hour. That is 12.4% below the average wage for retail workers even after adjusting for geography, according to a recent study by Arindrajit Dube and Steve Wertheim, economists at the University of California's Institute of Industrial Relations and long-time Wal-Mart researchers. Wal-Mart's wages are nearly 15% below the average wage of workers at large retailers and about 30% below the average wage of unionized grocery workers. The average U.S. wage is $17.80 an hour; Costco, a direct competitor of Wal-Mart's Sam's Club warehouse stores, pays an average wage of $16 an hour (see box on p. 32).

Wal-Mart may be improving its benefits, as the *Journal*'s editors report, but it needs to. Other retailers provide health care coverage to over 53% of their workers, while Wal-Mart covers just 48% of its workers. Costco, once again, does far better, covering 82% of its employees. Moreover, Wal-Mart's coverage is far less comprehensive than the plans offered by other large retailers. Dube reports that according to 2003 IRS data, Wal-Mart paid 59% of the health care costs of its workers and dependents, compared to the 77% of health care costs for individuals and 68% for families the average retailer picks up.

A recent internal Wal-Mart memo leaked to the *New York Times* confirmed the large gaps in Wal-Mart's health care coverage and exposed the high costs those gaps impose on government programs. According to the memo, "Five percent of our Associates are on Medicaid compared to an average for national employees of 4 percent. Twenty-seven percent of Associates' children are on such programs, compared to a national average of 22 percent. In total, 46 percent of Associates' children are either on Medicaid or are uninsured."

A considerably lower 29% of children of all large-retail workers are on Medicaid or are uninsured. Some 7% of the children of employees of large retailers go uninsured, compared to the 19% reported by Wal-Mart.

Wal-Mart's low wages drag down the wages of other retail workers and shutter downtown retail businesses. A 2005 study by David Neumark, Junfu Zhang, and Stephen Ciccarella, economists at the University of California at Irvine, found that Wal-Mart adversely affects employment and wages. Retail workers in a community with a Wal-Mart earned 3.5% less because Wal-Mart's low prices force other businesses to lower prices, and hence their wages, according to the Neumark study. The same study also found that Wal-Mart's presence reduces retail employment by 2% to 4%. While other studies have not found this negative employment effect, Dube's research also reports fewer retail jobs and lower wages for retail workers in metropolitan counties with a Wal-Mart. (Fully 85% of Wal-Mart stores are in metropolitan counties.) Dube figures that Wal-Mart's presence costs retail workers, at Wal-Mart and elsewhere, $4.7 billion a year in lost earnings.

In short, Wal-Mart's "everyday low prices" come at the expense of the compensation of Wal-Mart's own employees and lower wages and fewer jobs for retail workers in the surrounding area. That much remains true no matter what weight we assign to each of the measures that Wal-Mart uses to keep its costs down: a just-in-time inventory strategy, its ability to use its size to pressure suppliers for large discounts, a routinized work environment that requires minimal training, and meager wages and benefits.

How Low are Wal-Mart's Everyday Low Prices?

Even if one doesn't subscribe to the editors' position that it is consumers, not Wal-Mart, who cause job losses at downtown retailers, it is possible to argue that the benefit of Wal-Mart's low prices to consumers, especially low-income consumers, outweighs the cost endured by workers at Wal-Mart and other retailers. Jason Furman, New York University economist and director of economic policy for the 2004 Kerry-Edwards campaign, makes just such an argument. Wal-Mart's "staggering" low prices are 8% to 40% lower than people would pay elsewhere, according to Furman. He calculates that those low prices on average boost low-income families' buying power by 3% and more than offset the loss of earnings to retail workers. For Furman, that makes Wal-Mart "a progressive success story."

But exactly how much savings Wal-Mart affords consumers is far from clear. Estimates vary widely. At one extreme is a study Wal-Mart itself commissioned by Global Insight, an economic forecasting firm. Global Insight estimates Wal-Mart created a stunning savings of $263 billion, or $2,329 per household, in 2004 alone.

At the other extreme, statisticians at the U.S. Bureau of Labor Statistics found no price savings at Wal-Mart. Relying on Consumer Price Index data, the BLS found that Wal-Mart's prices largely matched those of its rivals, and that instances of lower prices at Wal-Mart could be attributed to lower quality products.

Both studies, which rely on the Consumer Price Index and aggregate data, have their critics. Furman himself allows that the Global Insight study is "overly simplistic" and says he "doesn't place as much weight on that one." Jerry Hausman, the M.I.T. economist who has looked closely at Wal-Mart's grocery stores, maintains that the CPI data that the Bureau of Labor Statistics relies on systematically miss the savings offered by "supercenters" such as Wal-Mart. To show the difference between prices at Wal-Mart and at other grocers, Hausman, along with Ephraim Leibtag, USDA Economic Research Service economist, used supermarket scanner data to examine the purchasing patterns of a national sample of 61,500 consumers from 1988 to 2001. Hausman and Leibtag found that Wal-Mart offers many identical food items at an average price about 15%-25% lower than traditional supermarkets.

While Hausman and Leibtag report substantial savings from shopping at Wal-Mart, they fall far short of the savings alleged in the Global Insight study. The Hausman and Leibtag study suggests a savings of around $550 per household per year, or about $56 billion in 2004, not $263 billion. Still, that is considerably more than the $4.7 billion a year in lost earnings to retail workers that Dube attributes to Wal-Mart.

But if "Wal-Mart hurts wages, not so much in retail, but across the whole country," as economist Neumark told *Business Week*, then the savings to consumers from Wal-Mart's everyday low prices might not outweigh the lost wages to all workers. (Retail workers make up just 11.6% of U.S. employment.)

Nor do these findings say anything about the sweatshop conditions and wages in Wal-Mart's overseas subcontractors. One example: A recent Canadian Broadcasting Corporation investigative report found that workers in Bangladesh were being paid less than $50 a month (below even the United Nation's $2 a day measure of poverty) to make clothes for the Wal-Mart private label, Simply Basic. Those workers included 10- to 13-year-old children forced to work long hours in dimly lit and dirty conditions sewing "I Love My Wal-Mart" t-shirts.

Making Wal-Mart Do Better

Nonetheless, as Arindrajit Dube points out, the relevant question is not whether Wal-Mart creates more savings for consumers than losses for workers, but whether the corporation can afford to pay better wages and benefits.

Dube reasons that if the true price gap between Wal-Mart and its retail competitors is small, then Wal-Mart might not be in a position to do better—to make up its wage and benefit gap and still maintain its price advantage. But if Wal-Mart offers consumers only minor price savings, then its lower wages and benefits hardly constitute a progressive success story that's good for the nation.

If Wal-Mart's true price gap is large (say, the 25% price advantage estimated by Hausman), then Wal-Mart surely is in a position to do better. For instance, Dube calculates that closing Wal-Mart's 16% overall compensation gap with other large retailers would cost the company less than 2% of sales. Raising prices by two cents on the dollar to cover those increased compensation costs would be "eminently absorbable," according to Dube, without eating away much of the company's mind-boggling $10 billion profit (2004).

Measures that set standards to force Wal-Mart and all big-box retailers to pay decent wages and provide benefits are beginning to catch on. Chicago, New York City, and the state of Maryland have considered or passed laws that would require big-box retailers to pay a "living wage" or to spend a minimum amount per worker-hour for health benefits. The Republican board of Nassau County on Long Island passed an ordinance requiring that all big-box retailers pay $3 per hour toward

The Costco Alternative?
Wall Street Prefers Wal-Mart

In an April 2004 online commentary, *Business Week* praised Costco's business model but pointed out that Costco's wages cause Wall Street to worry that the company's "operating expenses could get out of hand." How does Costco compare to low-wage Wal-Mart on overhead expenses? At Costco, overhead is 9.8% of revenue; at Wal-Mart, it is 17%. Part of Costco's secret is that its better paid workers are also more efficient: Costco's operating profit per hourly employee is $13,647; each Wal-Mart employee only nets the company $11,039. Wal-Mart also spends more than Costco on hiring and training new employees: each one, according to Rutgers economist Eileen Appelbaum, costs the company $2,500 to $3,500. Appelbaum estimates that Wal-Mart's relatively high turnover costs the company $1.5 to $2 million per year.

Despite Costco's higher efficiency, Wall Street analysts like Deutsche Bank's Bill Dreher complain that "Costco's corporate philosophy is to put its customers first, then its employees, then its vendors, and finally its shareholders. Shareholders get the short end of the stick." Wall Street prefers Wal-Mart's philosophy: executives first, then shareholders, then customers, then vendors, and finally employees.

Average Hourly Wage		Percentage of U.S. Workforce in Unions		Employees Covered by Company Health Insurance		Employees Who Leave After One Year	
Wal-Mart	Costco	Wal-Mart	Costco	Wal-Mart	Costco	Sam's Club*	Costco
$9.68	$16.00	0.0%	17.9%	48%	82%	21%	6%

* Sam's Club is the Wal-Mart unit that competes directly with Costco.

In 2004, Wal-Mart paid CEO Lee Scott $5.3 million, while a full-time employee making the average wage would have received $20,134. Costco's CEO Jim Senegal received $350,000, while a full-time average employee got $33,280. And *Business Week* intimates that the top job at Costco may be tougher than at Wal-Mart. "Management has to hustle to make the high-wage strategy work. It's constantly looking for ways to repackage goods into bulk items, which reduces labor, speeds up Costco's just-in-time inventory, and boosts sales per square foot. Costco is also savvier ... about catering to small shop owners and more affluent customers, who are more likely to buy in bulk and purchase higher-margin goods."

Costco's allegedly more affluent clientele may be another reason that its profit per employee is higher than Wal-Mart's and its overhead costs a lower percentage of revenue. However, Costco pays its employees enough that they could afford to shop there. As the *Business Week* commentary noted, "the low-wage approach cuts into consumer spending and, potentially, economic growth."

—Esther Cervantes

health care. Wal-Mart's stake in making sure that such proposals don't become law or spread nationwide goes a long way toward explaining why 80% of Wal-Mart's $2 million in political contributions in 2004 went to Republicans.

Henry Ford sought to pay his workers enough so they could buy the cars they produced. Sam Walton sought to pay his workers so little that they could afford to shop nowhere else. And while what was good for the big automakers was probably never good for the nation, what is good for Wal-Mart, today's largest employer, is undoubtedly bad for economic justice.

John Miller teaches economics at Wheaton College and is a member of the D&S *collective. Esther Cervantes is business and circulation manager at* D&S.

Sources: "Is Wal-Mart Good for America?" *Wall Street Journal*, 12/3/05; "Gauging the Wal-Mart Effect," *WSJ*, 12/03/05; Arindrajit Dube & Steve Wertheim, "Wal-Mart and Job Quality—What Do We Know, and Should We Care?" 10/05; Jason Furman, "Wal-Mart: A Progressive Success Story," 10/05; Leo Hindery Jr., "Wal-Mart's Giant Sucking Sound," 10/05; A. Bernstein, "Some Uncomfortable Findings for Wal-Mart," *Business Week Online*, 10/26/05, and "Wal-Mart: A Case for the Defense, Sort of," *Business Week Online*, 11/7/05; Dube, Jacobs, and Wertheim, "The Impact of Wal-Mart Growth on Earnings throughout the Retail Sector in Urban and Rural Counties," *Institute of Industrial Relations Working Paper*, U-C Berkeley, 10/05; Dube, Jacobs, and Wertheim, "Internal Wal-Mart Memo Validates Findings of UC Berkeley Study," 11/26/05; Jerry Hausman and Ephraim Leibtag, "Consumer Benefits from Increased Competition in Shopping Outlets: Measuring the Effect of Wal-Mart," 10/05; Hausman and Leibtag, "CPI Bias from Supercenters: Does the BLS Know that Wal-Mart Exists?" *NBER Working Paper No. 10712*, 8/04; David Neumark, Junfu Zhang, and Stephen Ciccarella, "The Effects of Wal-Mart on Local Labor Markets," *NBER Working Paper No. 11782*, 11/05; Erin Johansson, "Wal-Mart: Rolling Back Workers' Wages, Rights, and the American Dream," (American Rights at Work, 11/05); Wal-Mart Watch, "Spin Cycle"; CBC News, "Wal-Mart to cut ties with Bangladesh factories using child labour," 11/30/05; National Labor Committee, "10 to 13-year-olds Sewing 'I Love My Wal-Mart' Shirts," 12/05; Global Insight, "The Economic Impact of Wal-Mart," 2005.

Article 12

HEALTH CARE SECURITY IN NYC

HANNAH CLARKE
November/December 2005

While companies in the airline and auto industries are doing their best to cut health benefits, something unusual has happened in New York City: businesses have joined with activists to fight for mandatory, employer-based health care. The Health Care Security Act, which passed the City Council in August on a 46 to 1 vote, requires large grocery stores to help pay for health care for all employees, including part-timers. It's an innovative program that could spread to other industries in New York, and to other cities around the country.

Under the new law, owners of grocery stores with 35 or more employees must contribute approximately $2.50 toward health care costs for each hour an employee works. Over 70 percent of grocery stores in New York already provide health coverage at that rate, organizers say. Stores can meet the requirement by insuring their workers, or they can contribute an equivalent amount to a medical savings account in the worker's name. Over 21,000 workers in large grocery stores already receive health care contributions from their employers at this rate; the new law extends coverage to an additional 6,000 workers in the sector. No one at the grocery stores contacted for this article returned calls seeking comment, and neither did the one City Council member who voted against the bill.

Jobs with Justice and the Brennan Center for Justice at the NYU School of Law began developing the legislation over two years ago to address declining employer-based health coverage. They started recruiting business owners early in the process, knowing industry support was crucial for the bill to pass. One early supporter was John Catsimatidis, owner of the grocery chain Gristedes, which has a fully unionized workforce.

"I believe in competition on an equal plane," Catsimatidis said in an interview. "Since all our workers in New York have health care, if stores like Wal-Mart were to come in from the outside, they should have to compete on a level playing field."

The bill initially covered a wide variety of industries like construction and janitorial services, none of which could move out of the city to escape the higher labor costs. Most employers in the targeted industries already insured their workers, so those that didn't couldn't argue it was unaffordable. In its original form, the bill received the endorsement of 12 trade associations and over 100 business owners, many of them construction or electrical contractors. "There was not really any vocal industry opposition," said Paul Sonn, associate counsel at the Brennan Center.

In their campaign, organizers frequently cited the fact that city and state governments pick up the tab for uninsured workers through entitlement programs like Medicaid. "They're using the public hospitals and the welfare rolls as their health insurance plan," said Pat Purcell, an organizer with United Food and Commercial Workers Local 1500. Sherry Glied, a health policy professor at Columbia, estimates that taxpayers and medical practitioners pay $612 million a year to provide health care to New Yorkers with jobs. At one press conference, organizers stacked up 612 burlap sacks—a vivid reminder of the costs of a low-wage economy.

Religious groups also signed on to help with the campaign. The health care committee at one synagogue, B'nai Jeshurun, invited City Council Speaker Gifford Miller, who hadn't yet voiced support for the bill, to talk with the congregation about it and other social causes. Over 700 people came, said Lauren Barker, an organizer with Jobs with Justice. "I think that really helped push him to see that there was huge support for this in the city."

Despite strong support from industry and the City Council, the bill was slimmed down to cover only food stores. That's partly because it could face a legal challenge; under ERISA (the Employee Retirement Income Security Act), the government can't require employers to insure their workers. But the Health Care Security Act lets businesses choose how to spend their $2.50 per worker per hour—whether in personal accounts or as insurance—so organizers think it can withstand a legal challenge. "The hope is that once it's successfully implemented and upheld by the courts, the Council will look into expanding it," Sonn said.

Hannah Clark is a writer based in New York City.

RESOURCES: The Brennan Center for Justice, NYU School of Law <www.brennancenter.org>; New York Jobs with Justice <www.nyjwj.org>.

Article 13

ILL AND INSOLVENT

Illness and medical bills trigger half of all personal bankruptcies, and private insurance offers little protection.

KAYTY HIMMELSTEIN
July/August 2005

This spring, Congress voted overwhelmingly to pass the Bankruptcy Abuse Prevention and Consumer Protection Act, which makes it harder for people to declare bankruptcy. President Bush hurriedly added his signature on April 20, saying, "America is a nation of personal responsibility where people are expected to meet their obligations." The law, a gift to the banking and credit card industries, imposes new restrictions on bankruptcy filing, including rigid rules for setting repayment schedules, mandatory credit counseling, and a predetermined formula (dubbed a "means test") that takes away judges' discretion in determining whether a person may file for bankruptcy at all.

The means test provision has alarmed legal scholars because it does not allow judges to take individual circumstances into consideration. As Harvard Law School Professor Elizabeth Warren testified to the Senate Judiciary Committee, "The means test as written … treats all families alike. … If Congress is determined to sort the good from the bad, then begin by sorting those who have been laid low by medical debts, those who lost their jobs, those whose breadwinners have been called to active duty and sent to Iraq, those who are caring for elderly parents and sick children from those few who overspend on frivolous purchases."

The new rule is especially worrisome in light of a recent study that found health care costs contributed to about half of America's 1.5 million bankruptcy filings in 2001. The study was coauthored by Elizabeth Warren, David Himmelstein, Deborah Thorne, and Steffie Woolhandler, and published in February 2005 on the website of the journal *Health Affairs*. The authors surveyed 1,771 people who filed for personal bankruptcy, conducting interviews with 931 of them. Nearly half (46.2%) of those surveyed met the authors' criteria for "major medical bankruptcy," and more than half (54.5%) met their broader criteria for "any medical bankruptcy" (see figure). Assuming the data are representative, 1.9 to 2.2 million Americans (filers and dependents) experienced some type of medical bankruptcy in 2001.

These are not by and large the uninsured. Three-fourths of medical debtors interviewed had health insurance at the onset of the illness. Many, however, faced lapses in coverage. One-third of those who had private insurance at first lost their coverage during the course of the illness. These gaps in coverage, tied primarily to unaffordable premiums and loss of employment, left debtors with enormous out-of-pocket expenses. Patients who lost private insurance racked up medical costs averaging $18,005 from hospital bills, prescription medicines, and doctor visits. Some who kept their insurance sank into debt nonetheless thanks to copayments and deductibles. In sum, private health insurance offers surprisingly little protection from bankruptcy, given involuntary interruptions in coverage and privately borne costs.

Illness triggered financial problems both directly, through medical costs, and indirectly, through lost income. Three-fifths (59.9%) of families bankrupted by medical problems said that bills from medical-care providers contributed to bankruptcy; 47.6% cited drug costs. Thirty-five percent had to curtail employment because of an illness, often to care for someone else. In the interviews, filers described the compounding effects of direct medical costs and indirect employment-related costs—for example, when an illness caused a job loss, which led to the loss of employment-based health coverage, or when parents of chronically ill children had to take time off from work, only to find that the simultaneous costs of the child's medical care and the loss of their income proved catastrophic.

The congressional debate over the bankruptcy bill focused on debtors who cheat the bankruptcy system and pass costs on to more responsible consumers, but the *Health Affairs* study paints a different picture. It shows that about half of those who file for bankruptcy do so because they or their family members have fallen ill or become injured in the context of a shredded health safety net. The new bankruptcy law wrongly treats all debtors as careless spendthrifts. It will make it far more difficult for hundreds of thousands forced by circumstance into overwhelming medical debt to regain their financial footing.

Katy Himmelstein is a former D&S *intern.*

Article 14

WAL-MART WELFARE

How taxpayers subsidize the world's largest retailer.

JENNA WRIGHT
January/February 2005

Wal-Mart has released its expansion plans for 2005, and Americans can expect up to 230 new supercenters to open in their communities. The company plans to open 50 million square feet of retail space this year. President and CEO Lee Scott is confident the expansion will boost Wal-Mart's bottom line. But it takes money to make money, and Wal-Mart is getting a surprising amount of that seed money, along with massive subsidies to its existing operations, from U.S. taxpayers.

A raft of studies show that millions of taxpayer dollars are flowing to new and existing Wal-Mart stores around the country. In many instances, individual Wal-Mart facilities have received either direct or indirect subsidies from states and localities. Last May, Good Jobs First (GJF), a research and advocacy group that seeks to hold corporations accountable when they receive public subsidies, released a report detailing subsidies Wal-Mart has received to build both retail stores and the network of nearly 100 distribution centers the company has created to facilitate its expansion. The group found that over 90% of the company's distribution centers have been subsidized. It also uncovered 91 instances when the retail stores received public funds, and believes "the real total is certainly much higher."

GJF investigators documented 244 Wal-Mart subsidy deals with a total value of $1.008 billion. Taxpayer dollars have helped individual stores and distribution centers with everything from free or cut-price land to general grants. One example: in Sharon Springs, N.Y., a distribution center made a deal with an industrial development agency for the agency to hold the legal title to the facility so the corporation could evade property taxes. Good Jobs First estimates that Wal-Mart will save about $46 million over the life of this one agreement.

Subsidizing Low Wages

Wal-Mart's low-road labor policies give the corporation access to a less obvious taxpayer subsidy: government benefits to its employees. The company's policies by now are notorious: wages at or close to poverty level, managers discouraged from awarding overtime, employees forced to work off the clock without pay and repeatedly denied their right to organize. The result is that many Wal-Mart employees are eligible for myriad forms of public assistance. In other words, by providing financial assistance in various forms to Wal-Mart employees, the federal and state governments are essentially subsidizing the corporation for its substandard wages and benefits.

Health care benefits represent one such subsidy. Wal-Mart's employee health coverage is minimal and expensive; little of the company's vast low-wage workforce is covered. Nationally, two-thirds of workers at large firms get health insurance from their employer. But at Wal-Mart, only 41% to 46% of employees use the company's health insurance, in large part because many of Wal-Mart's low-wage workers simply cannot afford to pay the high premium the company charges. In 2001, Wal-Mart workers paid 42% of the total cost of the company's health plan. In contrast, the typical large business expects employees to pay only 16% of the total cost for individual coverage, or 25% for family coverage. At discount retailer Costco, which competes directly with Wal-Mart's Sam's Club stores, employees pay less than 10%; as a result, 82% of them are covered through the company.

Instead of providing affordable health insurance, Wal-Mart encourages its employees to sign up for publicly funded programs, dodging its health care costs and passing them on to taxpayers. The company is the poster child for a problem outlined in a 2003 AFL-CIO report on Wal-Mart's role in the health care crisis: "federal, state and local governments—American taxpayers—must pick up the multi-billion-dollar tab for employees and dependents, especially children, of large and profitable employers who are forced to rely on public hospitals and other public health programs for care and treatment they need but cannot obtain under their employers' health plans."

In Georgia, one of every four Wal-Mart employees has a child in the state's PeachCare health program, according to a recent survey. Over 10,000 of the 166,000 children covered by PeachCare have a parent working for Wal-Mart; no other employer in the state has a comparable share of its employees in the program.

In California, the families of Wal-Mart employees use an estimated 40% more in publicly funded health care than the average for families of employees at other large retail firms, according to an August 2003 study by University of California, Berkeley's Institute for Industrial Relations. Providing health care to Wal-Mart families costs California taxpayers an estimated $32 million annually.

Thanks to their poverty-level wages, Wal-Mart workers are often eligible for other kinds of government assistance as well. The same study found that California Wal-Mart employees and their families utilize an additional $54 million in non-health related federal assistance, including food stamps, the Earned Income Tax Credit, subsidized school lunches, and subsidized housing.

The Democratic staff of the House Committee on Education and the Workforce estimated the breakdown of costs for one 200-employee Wal-Mart store:

- $36,000 a year for free or reduced school lunches, assuming that 50 families of employees qualify.
- $42,000 a year for Section 8 rental assistance, assuming that 3% of the store employees qualify.
- $125,000 a year for federal tax credits and deductions for low-income families, assuming that 50 employees are heads of households with a child, and 50 employees are married with two children.
- $108,000 a year for the additional federal contribution to state children's health insurance programs, assuming that 30 employees with an average of two children qualify.
- $100,000 a year for additional Title I expenses, assuming 50 families with two children qualify.
- $9,750 a year for the additional costs of low-income energy assistance.

Overall, the committee estimates that one 200-person Wal-Mart store may result in an excess cost of $420,750 a year for federal taxpayers.

The effects of Wal-Mart's free-loader policies radiate beyond Wal-Mart itself; Wal-Mart employees are not the only victims. Firms large and small are forced to cut their own costs in order to compete, creating a "race to the bottom, in which everyone suffers," according to the AFL-CIO report. Employers that provide adequate pay and benefits to their employees are under pressure from companies like Wal-Mart that do not. The result: a growing low-wage sector and ever-greater need for government benefits (funded, incidentally, by an increasingly regressive tax structure).

As an economic power, Wal-Mart is in a class by itself, with over $8 billion in net income last year—it's about five times the size of the second-largest retailer in the United States. Wal-Mart's sheer size means it can drag whole sectors with millions of workers both in the United States and abroad down its low-road path. Taxpayers are feeding this giant corporate monster, and at a very high price.

Jenna Wright is a former D&S intern.

SOURCES: Democratic Staff of the Committee on Education and the Workforce, U.S. House of Representatives, "Everyday Low Wages: The Hidden Price We All Pay for Wal-Mart," February 16, 2004; AFL-CIO, "Wal-Mart: An Example of Why Workers Remain Uninsured and Underinsured,"

October 2003; Philip Mattera and Anna Purinton, "Shopping for Subsidies: How Wal-Mart Uses Taxpayer Money to Finance Its Never-Ending Growth," (Good Jobs First, May 2004); Labor Research Association, "Low Wage Nation," 2004.

Article 15

ABCs OF AIDS PREVENTION

Uganda has been widely recognized for its successes in stemming the AIDS crisis, but its policies fail to address the inequalities that make women vulnerable to the disease.

JESSICA WEISBERG
January/February 2005

Uganda is one of a handful of countries to have dramatically reduced its overall HIV infection rate in the past 10 years. It's widely viewed as a global leader in AIDS policy and is seen as a model for other countries in Africa and the global South. Its approach, known as "ABC," stands for "Abstinence, Be faithful, and Condoms"—but critics refer to it as "A-B-and sometimes-C" because of policymakers' emphasis on the first two over the third.

Despite Uganda's notable successes in stemming the AIDS epidemic, ABC has serious limitations. The policy primarily targets male behavior and fails to protect a particularly vulnerable population: married women. It offers little to girls forced by poverty to exchange one of their only assets—their bodies—for basic necessities or school fees. And by focusing on prevention, the policy fails to expand affordable and available treatments to those who've already contracted the disease—or address the core economic and social inequalities that make women susceptible to infection.

Nevertheless, President Bush has routinely cited Uganda's emphasis on abstinence and fidelity in defending its own abstinence-oriented global initiatives. In fact, the United States has adopted the ABC model as the centerpiece of its international AIDS policy.

In his 2004 State of the Union address, Bush declared optimistically, "AIDS can be prevented." Prevented? AIDS can be *treated*; with anti-retroviral therapies, widely available since early 1996, the otherwise fatal illness takes on a chronic character. By prevention, the president was referring not to a vaccine but to abstinence. He's been known to say it "works every time."

A few months after the address, in May 2004, Congress passed the President's Emergency Plan for AIDS Relief (PEPFAR). It allocated $15 billion dollars for AIDS programs worldwide over five years, with a focus on 15 "target countries" which are home to more than 50% of all people with HIV: Botswana, Côte d'Ivoire, Ethiopia, Kenya, Mozambique, Namibia, Nigeria, Rwanda, South Africa, Tanzania, Uganda, Zambia, Vietnam, Guyana, and Haiti.

Twenty percent of PEPFAR funding will go to prevention programs. (The balance goes to support services and treatment.) By law, at least one-third of those prevention funds must be used to promote abstinence. The first allocation of $100 million in PEPFAR grants for abstinence programs was announced in October. Nine of the 11 organizations that won the grants were faith-based organizations. Under PEPFAR, such groups are allowed to exclude information about contraception from their educational programs. Ambassador Randall Tobias, head of the State Department's Office of Global AIDS, has cited Uganda's accomplishments when PEPFAR's abstinence program has faced questions.

Uganda's Way

Since Ugandan President Yoweri Museveni initiated the ABC program in the mid-1990s, the country has undergone enormous reductions in HIV prevalence (the percentage of individuals living with HIV/AIDS). The percent of infected individuals in Uganda has declined from around 30% in the early 1990s to 6% in 2004, according to the United Nations and the Ugandan government. Although some scientists question the validity of those specific figures, arguing that survey methodology is flawed and that the reduction in prevalence rates may in part reflect the deaths of those who had HIV in the 1990s, most agree that Uganda has secured the most dramatic turnaround in AIDS of any country to date. Museveni brought this about by aggressively raising AIDS awareness, by using radio and other modes of mass communication, involving churches and nongovernmental organizations, and by crafting messages that resonated with Ugandan culture; for example, he introduced the slogan "zero grazing" to encourage monogamy in the cattle-oriented society.

The effectiveness of Uganda's AIDS prevention and treatment policies has varied, though, with respect to gender. Far more women than men have become infected with HIV since ABC was implemented. According to the Uganda AIDS Commission, there were 99,031 new HIV cases in the country in 2001. Of these, females were three to six times more likely to become infected by HIV than males in the 15 to 19 age bracket, according to the Uganda Women's Network. In the 20 to 24 age bracket, the HIV infection rate among women remains twice as high as that of men.

There are several reasons for this disparity. Most importantly, research indicates that marriage actually *increases* the chance of HIV infection. In fact, the most dramatic increase in prevalence rates in recent years has occurred among monogamous married women; even as the overall percentage of people with HIV has fallen, the percentage of married women with HIV has increased. One study found that in rural Uganda, 88% of HIV-infected women age 15 to 19 are married.

For the majority of married couples in Uganda, the woman is at least six years younger than her husband. Paul Zeitz of the advocacy group Global AIDS Alliance points out that abstinence programs could "in effect be encouraging women to marry earlier," placing them at risk of infection by older husbands. "What use is abstinence, what use is fidelity if he is already infected and brings it into the marriage?" Stephen Lewis asked the *Agence France Presse*. Zeitz goes so far as to argue: "Abstinence [promotion] could be leading to a public health crisis."

Take Suzan, a 17-year-old mother from Ndeeba, a Kampala suburb, whose

62-year-old husband recently died of AIDS. She was infected by her late husband, and is unable to afford treatment.

With such large age differences between wives and husbands, Ugandan women like Suzan often outlive their husbands. When a man dies, his family typically repossesses his assets, robbing the woman of all her property and making her remaining years all the more difficult. In Suzan's case, her husband's family has taken away both their land and her child.

Another Ugandan woman, Juliet, is a 27-year-old widow with four children. Her in-laws also took away her home and land upon her husband's death. She is now hospitalized with an advanced case of AIDS, and her children are struggling to support themselves.

Women like Suzan and Juliet are overlooked by the ABC program's emphasis on abstinence and fidelity. Both women were abstinent before marriage and then faithful, but neither their own behavior nor the ABC program did anything to protect them from contracting the disease or to treat them once they were infected.

Condoms too are of little use to married women in a culture where extramarital polygamy is common but wives are unaware of their husbands' affairs. Even if women have suspicions, many adhere to patriarchal mores against vocally questioning their husbands' behavior. Those same mores also deter women from telling their husbands to wear condoms.

Harriet Abwoli, interviewed in 2003 for the Human Rights Watch report "Just Die Quietly," described her experience: "He used to force me to have sex with him. He would beat me and slap me when I refused. I never used a condom with him. ... When I got pregnant I went for a medical check-up. When I gave birth, and the child had passed away, they told me I was HIV-positive. I cried. The doctor told me, 'Wipe your tears, the whole world is sick.'"

"Women do not have negotiation power," says researcher Sarah Kalloch, who has done considerable fieldwork in Uganda. "Women do not have control over their own bodies." Kalloch describes instances of wife-swapping, wife inheritance, and widespread marital rape. Rape and domestic violence are "virtually impossible to prosecute" due to legal discrimination. "ABC is not enough for women in Uganda. They need legal rights that give them control over their bodies, their relationships, and who they marry," Kalloch says.

They also need basic economic security. Uganda's abstinence program has attempted to reach "high risk" populations such as soldiers and truck drivers, but has sent mixed messages by disparaging female HIV victims for indulgent or "promiscuous" behavior. So long as extreme economic deprivation continues to force young girls to barter for food and basic economic needs with sex, this sort of message will do little to save those who lack access to income and resources.

In the poverty-stricken northern region of Uganda, it's common for parents to force their teen and pre-teen daughters into sex work. "The mother will simply say to her daughters, 'come back with food,'" said Paul Zeitz of Global AIDS Alliance. Zeitz refers to this practice as "survival sex," since selling sex is not a profession for most of these girls, but a measure driven by dire economic necessity. Most customers are truck drivers and traveling soldiers, who prefer young girls, believing that they are free of HIV. Truck drivers synchronize their routes with school tuition deadlines (which vary by region), when girls are most likely to be waiting at truck stops for customers, according to a study conducted by the group.

When asked if abstinence programs fail women, Randall Tobias said, "One of the best ways to protect vulnerable women from HIV is to instill the 'ABC' message in men...." To Tobias, "the ABC model is a simple conceptualization of the major tenets of what happened in Uganda and can be implemented elsewhere with some local adaptation."

But as Lynn Amowitz, a Harvard medical school professor who has researched women's health and human rights in Afghanistan, observes: "The forms discrimination and stigma take differ from country to country. In some places, it's widow inheritance, in others it's that women are considered minors." Extending abstinence programs to these countries, with their distinct social dynamics, is unlikely to slow the feminization of HIV and AIDS. Without specific prevention programs that take such practices into account, the burden of HIV/AIDS will continue to disproportionately affect women.

Already, 58% of the 25 million people living with AIDS in sub-Saharan Africa are women. Adult women are up to 1.3 times more likely to be infected with HIV than their male counterparts, and women and girls now make up three-quarters of the 6.2 million young people (age 15 to 24) with AIDS. Because women serve as the primary caregivers for their own children and work in disproportionate numbers in schools, as nurses, and in social services, the feminization of AIDS ravages the socioeconomic fabric of their communities. Furthermore, the epidemic will be passed on to future generations, as the likelihood of mother-to-child transmission is estimated at 30%.

Treatment Possibilities

The situation is not hopeless. Life-extending drugs such as nevaripine and anti-retroviral therapies do exist. The World Health Organization (WHO) has engineered generic anti-retrovirals that will reduce the cost of therapy to $148 dollars a year, compared to an average $548 a year for name-brand drugs.

But the Bush administration has put the breaks on treatment. Under PEPFAR, all drugs sold abroad must be approved by the FDA. Even generic drugs that have already undergone the WHO's meticulous prequalification standards must be reexamined by the FDA before they are distributed abroad through the program. This rule will indefinitely delay the availability of affordable medication.

What's more, PEPFAR allocates no funds for distributing nevaripine, which at a cost of $4 per person can reduce the likelihood of mother-to-child transmission by almost 90%. Likewise, it does not fund the development of microbicides, topical products that women could use, undetected, to prevent sexual transmission of HIV. Protesters at the International AIDS Conference in Bangkok last July condemned Ambassador Tobias and President Bush for prioritizing pharmaceutical patent rights over public health needs and ideology over efficacy.

Women's economic marginalization is a global problem, and severe in the 15 countries that PEPFAR will target. President Bush's vague declaration that "AIDS can be prevented" is, in fact, correct. Prevention programs can provide a cost-effective means of gradually reducing HIV prevalence, but only if such programs address specific economic inequities that underlie patterns of transmission, dismantle barriers to economic independence for women, empower married women, and deliver messages in a culturally accessible manner. Just as important, they cannot ignore the necessity of investing in treatment for women and their daughters, who are already infected. Otherwise, women's social and economic powerlessness will continue to render them disproportionately vulnerable to the HIV epidemic. For women, the solution to the AIDS crisis is a lot more complicated than A-B-C.

Jessica Weisberg is a former D&S intern.

RESOURCES: "The ABC Debate Heats Up," *Africa News*, July 13, 2004; Lisa Garbus and Elliot Marseille, *Country AIDS Analysis Project: HIV/AIDS in Uganda*, San Francisco: AIDS Policy Research Center, University of California San Francisco, 2003; "Health: Women Demand Stepped-Up AIDS Treatment, Prevention," Inter Press Service, 2002; Richard Ingham, "U.N. Envoy Blasts U.S. for "Ideological Agenda" on Abstinence to Combat AIDS," Agence France Presse, Bangkok, July 15, 2004; "Just Die Quietly," Human Rights Watch, 2003; Alonso Luiza Klein, "Women's Social Representation of Sex, Sexuality, and AIDS in Brazil," *Women's Experiences with HIV/AIDS: An International Perspective*. New York: Columbia University Press, 1996; Catherine Ntabade, "Abolish Polygamy," The Uganda Women's Network; Sharon Otterman, "AIDS: The U.S. Anti-AIDS Program," Council of Foreign Relations, November 28, 2003; www.siecus.org/policy/PUpdates/pdate0073.html; "Uganda Puts Morality Before Condoms," Global News Wire, July 15, 2004.

Article 16

AFRICAN AMERICANS AND SOCIAL SECURITY
Why the privatization advocates are wrong.

WILLIAM E. SPRIGGS
November/December 2004

Proponents of Social Security privatization are trying to claim that the current program is unfair to African Americans and that a privatized program would serve African Americans better. This argument lends support to the privatization agenda while at the same time giving its advocates a compassionate gloss. But the claims about African Americans and Social Security are wrong.

The Old Age Survivors and Disability Insurance Program (OASDI), popularly known as Social Security, was put in place by Franklin Roosevelt to establish a solid bulwark of economic rights for the public—specifically, as he put it, "the right to adequate protection from the economic fears of old age, sickness, accident, and unemployment." Most Americans associate Social Security only with the retirement—

or old age—benefit. Yet it was created to do much more, and it does.

As its original name suggests, Social Security is an insurance program that protects workers and their families against the income loss that occurs when a worker retires, becomes disabled, or dies. All workers will eventually either grow too old to compete in the labor market, become disabled, or die. OASDI insures all workers and their families against these universal risks, while spreading the costs and benefits of that insurance protection among the entire workforce. Currently, 70% of Social Security funds go to retirees, 15% to disabled workers, and 15% to survivors.

Social Security is a "pay as you go" system, which means the taxes paid by today's workers are not set aside to pay their own benefits down the road, but rather go to pay the benefits of current Social Security recipients. It's financed using the Federal Insurance Contribution Act (or FICA) payroll tax, paid by all working Americans on earnings of less than about $90,000 a year. While the payroll tax is not progressive, Social Security benefits are—that is, low-wage workers receive a greater percentage of pre-retirement earnings from the program than higher-wage workers.

In the 1980s, recognizing that the baby boom generation would strain this system, Congress passed reforms to raise extra tax revenues above and beyond the current need and set up a trust fund to hold the reserve. Trustees were appointed and charged with keeping Social Security solvent. Today's trustees warn that their projections, which are based on modest assumptions about the long-term growth of the U.S. economy, show the system could face a shortfall around 2042, when either benefits would have to be cut or the FICA tax raised.

Those who oppose the social nature of the program have pounced on its projected shortfall in revenues to argue that the program cannot—or ought not—be fixed, but should instead be fundamentally changed (see "Privatization Advocates.") Privatization proponents are seeking to frame the issue as a matter of social justice, as if Social Security "reform" would primarily benefit low-income workers, blue-collar workers, people of color, and women. Prompted by disparities in life expectancy between whites and African Americans and the racial wealth gap, a growing chorus within the privatization movement is claiming that privatizing Social Security would be beneficial to African Americans.

Opponents attack the program on the basis of an analogy to private retirement accounts. Early generations of Social Security beneficiaries received much more in benefits than they had paid into the system in taxes. Privatization proponents argue those early recipients received a "higher rate of return" on their "investment" while current and future generations are being "robbed" because they will see "lower rates of return." They argue the current system of social insurance—particularly the retirement program—should be privatized, switching from the current "pay-as-you-go" system to one in which individual workers claim their own contribution and decide where and how to invest it.

But this logic inverts the premise of social insurance. Rather than sharing risk across the entire workforce to ensure that all workers and their families are protected from the three inevitabilities of old age, disability, and death, privatizing Social Security retirement benefits would enable high-wage workers to reap gains from private retirement investment without having to help protect lower-wage workers from their (disproportionate) risks of disability and death. High-wage workers, who are more likely to live long enough to retire, could in fact do better on average if they opt out of the general risk pool and devote all their money to retirement without having to cover the risk of those who may become disabled or die, although they would of course be subjecting their retirement dollars to greater risk. But low-wage workers, who are far more likely to need disability or survivors' benefits to help their families and are less likely to live long enough to retire, would then be left with lower disability and survivors' benefits, and possibly no guaranteed benefits. This is what the Social Security privatization movement envisions. But you wouldn't know it from reading their literature.

And when the myths about Social Security's financial straits meet another American myth—race—even more confusion follows. Here is a look at three misleading claims by privatization proponents about African Americans and Social Security.

Myth #1

Several conservative research groups argue that Social Security is a bad deal for African Americans because of their lower life expectancies. "Lifetime Social Security benefits depend, in large part, on longevity," writes the Cato Institute's Michael Tanner in his briefing paper "Disparate Impact: Social Security and African Americans." "At every age, African-American men and women both have shorter life expectancies than do their white counterparts. ... As a result, a black man or woman earning exactly the same lifetime wages, and paying exactly the same lifetime Social Security taxes, as his or her white counterpart will likely receive a far lower rate of return." Or as the Americans for Tax Reform web site puts it: "A black male born today has a life expectancy of 64.8 years. But the Social Security retirement age for that worker in the future will be 67 years. That means probably the majority of black males will never even receive Social Security retirement benefits."

The longevity myth is the foundation of all the race-based arguments for Social Security privatization. There are several problems with it.

First, the shorter life expectancy of African Americans compared to whites is the result of higher morbidity in mid-life, and is most acute for African-American men. The life expectancies of African-American women and white men are virtually equal. So the life expectancy argument can really only be made about African-American men.

Second, the claim that OASDI is unfair to African Americans because their expected benefits are less than their expected payments is usually raised and then answered from the perspective of the retirement (or "old age") benefit alone. That is an inaccurate way to look at the problem. Because OASDI also serves families of workers who become disabled or die, a correct measure would take into account the probability of all three risk factors—old age, disability, and death. Both survivor benefits and disability benefits, in fact, go disproportionately to African Americans.

While African Americans make up 12% of the U.S. population, 23% of children receiving Social Security survivor benefits are African American, as are about 17% of disability beneficiaries. On average, a worker who receives disability benefits or a family that receives survivor benefits gets far more in return than the worker paid in FICA taxes, notwithstanding privatizers' attempts to argue that Social Security is a bad deal.

Survivors' benefits also provide an important boost to poor families more generally. A recent study by the National Urban League Institute for Opportunity and Equality showed that the benefit lifted 1 million children out of poverty and helped another 1 million avoid extreme poverty (living below half the poverty line).

Finally, among workers who do live long enough to get the retirement benefit, life expectancies don't differ much by racial group. For example, at age 65, the life expectancies of African-American and white men are virtually the same.

President Bush's Social Security commission proposed the partial privatization of Social Security retirement accounts, but cautioned that it could not figure out how to maintain equal benefits for the other risk pools. The commission suggested that disability and survivor's benefits would have to be reduced if the privatization plan proceeds.

This vision is of a retirement program designed for the benefit of the worker who retires—only. A program with that focus would work against, not for, African Americans because of the higher morbidity rates in middle age and the smaller share of African Americans who live to retirement.

Myth #2

African Americans have less education, and so are in the work force longer than whites, and yet Social Security only credits 35 years of work experience in figuring benefits. Tanner says, "benefits are calculated on the basis of the highest 35 years of earnings over a worker's lifetime. Workers must still pay Social Security taxes during years outside those 35, but those taxes do not count toward or earn additional benefits. Generally, those low-earnings years occur early in an individual's life. That is particularly important to African Americans because they are likely to enter the workforce at an earlier age than whites.…"

This claim misinterprets the benefit formula for Social Security. Yes, African Americans on average are slightly less educated than whites. The gap is mostly because of a higher college completion rate for white men compared to African-American men. But the education argument fails to acknowledge that white teenagers have a significantly higher labor force participation rate (at 46%) than do African-American teens (29%). The higher labor force participation of white teenagers helps to explain why young white adults do better in the labor market than young African-American adults. (The racial gaps in unemployment are considerably greater for teenagers and young adults than for those over 25.)

These differences in early labor market experiences mean that African-American men have more years of zero earnings than do whites. So while the statement about education is true, the inference from education differences to work histories is false. By taking only 35 years of work history into account in the benefit formula, the Social Security formula is progressive. It in effect ignores years of zero or very low earnings. This levels the playing field among long-time workers, putting African Americans with more years of zero earnings on par with whites. By contrast, a private system based on total years of earnings would exacerbate racial labor market disparities.

Myth #3

A third claim put forward by critics of Social Security is that African-American retirees are more dependent on Social Security than whites. Tanner writes: "Elderly African Americans are much more likely than their white counterparts to be dependent on Social Security benefits for most or all of their retirement income." Therefore, he concludes, "African Americans would be among those with the most to gain from the privatization of Social Security—transforming the program into a system of individually owned, privately invested accounts." Law professor and senior policy advisor to Americans for Tax Reform Peter Ferrara adds, "the personal accounts would produce far higher returns and benefits for lower-income workers, African Americans, Hispanics, women and other minorities."

It's true that African-American retirees are more likely than whites to rely on Social Security as their only income in old age. It's the sole source of retirement income for 40% of elderly African Americans. This is a result of discrimination in the labor market that limits the share of African Americans with jobs that offer pension benefits. Privatizing Social Security would not change labor market discrimination or its effects.

Privatizing Social Security would, however, exacerbate the earnings differences between African Americans and whites, since benefits would be based solely on individual savings. What would help African-American retirees is not privatization, but rather changing the redistributive aspects of Social Security to make it even more progressive.

The current formula for Social Security benefits is progressive in two ways: low earners get a higher share of their earnings than do higher wage earners and the lowest years of earning are ignored. Changes in the formula to raise the benefits floor enough to lift all retired Social Security recipients out of poverty would make it still more progressive. Increasing and updating the Supplemental Security Income payment, which helps low earners, could accomplish the same goal for SSI recipients. (SSI is a program administered by Social Security for very low earners and the poor who are disabled, blind, or at least 65 years old.)

Privatization Advocates

Powerful advocates for privatization include libertarian and conservative think tanks and advocacy groups such as the Cato Institute, the Heritage Foundation, Americans for Tax Reform, and Citizens for a Sound Economy, all driven by an ideological commitment to the abolition of federal social programs.

Wall Street too is thirsty for the $1.4 trillion that privatization would funnel into equities if the taxes collected to support the Social Security system were invested privately rather than reinvested in federal government bonds. That's not to mention the windfall of fees privatization would deliver for banks, brokerage houses, and investment firms.

Just after he took office, President Bush appointed a commission to examine privatizing the Social Security system. The commission could not figure out how to maintain payments to current recipients while diverting tax dollars to the savings of current workers, nor could it resolve how to cover the benefits of the disabled or resolve issues surrounding survivors' benefits. Although the president did not succeed in carrying out Social Security privatization in his first term, he has made the partial privatization of Social Security retirement accounts the top priority of his second-term domestic agenda.

The proponents of privatization argue that the heavy reliance of African-American seniors on Social Security requires higher rates of return—returns that are only possible by putting money into the stock market. Yet given the lack of access to private pensions for African-American seniors and their low savings from lifetimes of low earnings, such a notion is perverse. It would have African Americans gamble with their only leg of retirement's supposed three-legged stool—pension, savings, and Social Security. And, given the much higher risk that African Americans face of both death before retirement and of disability, it would be a risky gamble indeed to lower those benefits while jeopardizing their only retirement leg.

Privatizing the retirement program, and separating the integrated elements of Social Security, would split America. The divisions would be many: between those more likely to be disabled and those who are not; between those more likely to die before retirement and those more likely to retire; between children who get survivors' benefits and the elderly who get retirement benefits; between those who retire with high-yield investments and those who fare poorly in retirement. The "horizontal equity" of the program (treating similar people in a similar way) would be lost, as volatile stock fluctuations and the timing of retirement could greatly affect individuals' rates of return. The "vertical equity" of the program (its progressive nature, insuring a floor for benefits) would be placed in greater jeopardy with the shift from social to private benefits.

Social Security works because it is "social." It is America's only universal federal program. The proposed changes would place Social Security in the same political space as the rest of America's federal programs—and African Americans have seen time and again how those politics work.

William E. Spriggs is a senior fellow at the Economic Policy Institute, and was the executive director of the National Urban League Institute for Opportunity and Equality.

Article 17

JOB-BASED HEALTH INSURANCE
Sick and Getting Sicker

JAMES WOOLMAN
May/June 2004

Job-based health insurance is terminally ill. A long-term decline in the percentage of workers who get health insurance through their jobs and a sharp rise in monthly costs are giving workers a bad case of "un-surance." They now bear more of the costs of medical care and are less certain than ever that their health benefits will be there in the future.

The pain has been acute since the recent economic downturn. A report from the Kaiser Family Foundation shows that employee contributions for health premiums increased a remarkable 50% between 2000 and 2003 (see Figure 1). In those three years, the percentage of private-sector workers who received insurance through their employers fell from 52% to 45%, according to the U.S. Labor Department (see Figure 2). Today, 80% of the nation's 44 million uninsured are in working families.

The current crisis is part of a long-term erosion in employee health benefits that dates back to the late 1970s. From 1983 to 2003, workers' monthly contributions for family health benefits, adjusted for inflation, almost quadrupled (see Figure 3). As costs shot up, the portion of private-sector workers covered through their jobs dwindled from two-thirds in 1983 to fewer than half in 2003.

Why the steep drop in job-based coverage? One reason is that the labor market has changed. Workers today are less likely to be in a union and more likely to work part time. In addition, more people work in the service sector, where employers often provide less generous health benefits than in manufacturing.

The other reason is that health insurance costs have exploded. Between 1980 and 2003, health care spending as a percent of gross domestic product increased from 9% to over 15%. Much of the cost inflation is driven by technological improvements and the increased use of health services. Another driver is the political influence of the powerful health care industry. Big Pharma's sway on Capitol Hill was

FIGURE 1
AVERAGE EMPLOYEE COSTS FOR HEALTH CARE 2000-2003*

	2000	2003	% Increase
Employee Portion of Annual Premium			
Single Coverage	$334	$508	52%
Family Coverage	$1,619	$2,412	49%
PPO Deductibles			
Preferred Provider	$175	$275	57%
Non-Preferred Provider	$340	$561	65%
Prescription Drug Co-Payments			
Preferred Drugs	$13	$19	46%
Non-Preferred Drugs	$17	$29	71%

*Includes public- and private-sector employees
Source: Kaiser Family Foundation, Employer Health Benefits Survey, 2003.
Note: Preferred Provider Organization (PPO) is a popular form of health plan. A PPO controls costs by contracting with "preferred" doctors. Patients receive the highest financial benefit if they see a preferred doctor. Patients are allowed to go "out of network," but bear more of the costs themselves if they do.

recently demonstrated by the passage of the Medicare drug bill in 2003, sections of which were virtually written by large pharmaceutical companies.

Current trends in job-based health benefits suggest that the future may be even bleaker for working people. Deductibles and co-payments, the fees individuals pay when they actually visit the doctor or purchase prescriptions, are the main source of growth in employee health care spending, aside from rising monthly premiums (see Figure 4).

Increasing these point-of-service costs is more than just another employer cost-shifting strategy.

Ratcheting up co-pays and deductibles is also a way for companies to limit the medical services that employees use. The higher the front-end costs to workers, the fewer total services used, and the lower the amount companies pay out for insurance. In effect, employers are using point-of-service fees to control overall costs.

Virtually all health care policy experts agree that some form of rationing is an inevitable part of any health care system. In countries with government-provided health insurance, the state allots care based on criteria like medical need and service availability. Similarly, managed care systems ration medical

FIGURE 2
PERCENT OF PRIVATE-SECTOR WORKERS RECEIVING JOB-BASED HEALTH INSURANCE

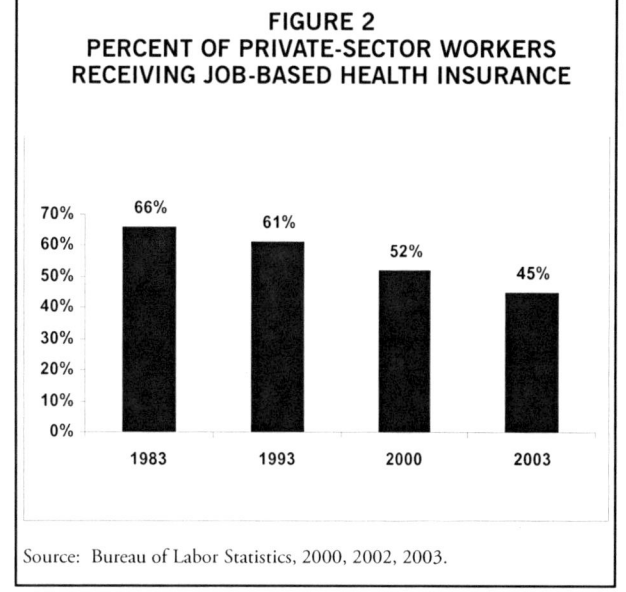

- 1983: 66%
- 1993: 61%
- 2000: 52%
- 2003: 45%

Source: Bureau of Labor Statistics, 2000, 2002, 2003.

FIGURE 2
AVERAGE MONTHLY EMPLOYEE CONTRIBUTION FOR HEALTH INSURANCE PREMIUMS, IN 2003 DOLLARS*

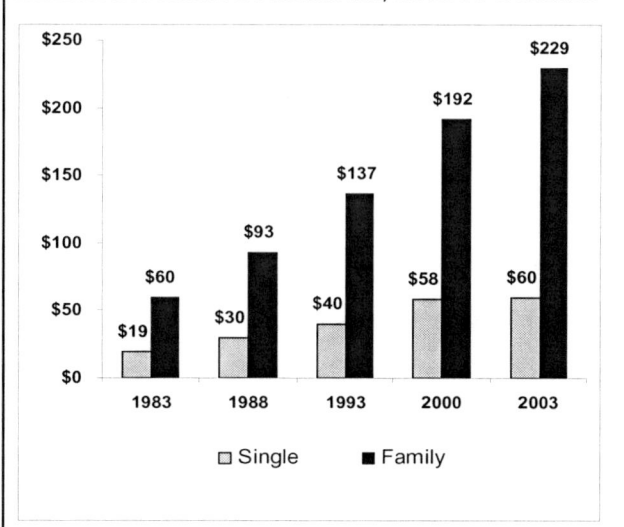

Year	Single	Family
1983	$19	$60
1988	$30	$93
1993	$40	$137
2000	$58	$192
2003	$60	$229

*Includes only private-sector employees.
Source: Bureau of Labor Statistics, 2001, 2002, 2003.

services according to rules that control costs—for example, by limiting access to specialists.

Pro-market policymakers and the insurance lobby decry the evils of government rationing, but in reality, U.S. employers already do ration care. Unlike a government health insurance system in which decisions about access to care are made based on fairness-related criteria, Americans' access to medical care is rationed by their ability to pay. The result? Seniors skip drug doses to make their prescriptions last longer and employees with high co-payments avoid going to the doctor because they have to pay the rent.

Most people in the United States don't think of medical care as a consumer good, but as a necessity to which everybody should have equal access. As prices rise and coverage shrinks, it might become something else altogether—a luxury item.

Figure 4
PERCENT OF PRIVATE SECTOR EMPLOYEES WITH INSURANCE AT WORK

	1999	2003
Union	73%	60%
Non-union	51%	44%
Goods-producing	69%	57%
Service-producing	48%	42%
Full-time	64%	56%
Part-time	14%	9%

Source: BLS Employee Benefits Survey, 1999, 2000, 2003

James Woolman is a graduate student at the John F. Kennedy School of Government and a Dollars & Sense *intern.*

RESOURCES: Americans For Health Care (SEIU); Kaiser Family Foundation, Employer Health Benefits Survey, 2003; Sally Trude, "Patient Cost Sharing: How Much is Too Much?" Center for Studying Health System Change, Issue Brief No. 72, December 2003; Bureau of Labor Statistics, "Employee Benefits in Private Industry, 2003" News Release, Sept. 17, 2003.

Article 18

HOME CARE WORKERS

Organizing victories in California, Oregon, and Washington.

STU SCHNEIDER

Thirteen thousand home care workers in Oregon voted overwhelmingly two years ago to join the Service Employees International Union (SEIU). The vote was the culmination of a four-year statewide campaign modeled on earlier efforts in Washington and California. "Twenty years of being unrecognized, underpaid, with no benefits, essentially an invisible workforce has made many of us frustrated and searching for solutions," Herk Mertens, a home care worker from Waldport, Oregon, told the Labor Research Association after the vote. "I honestly feel the union is the only way homecare workers and our clients have the ability to be visible, to have a voice decision-makers will hear and to press for improvements in quality of care and working conditions."

Home care workers bathe, clean, and feed the frail elderly and individuals with physical disabilities. They assist their clients at the toilet and transfer them into bed. Their work is physically and emotionally demanding, but essential in a society with an aging population and a poor and costly nursing-home system. Their efforts enable home care consumers to live independently within their homes and communities.

Despite their importance, home care workers are among the most underpaid workers in the United States. Predominantly women of color, they typically earn minimum wage or just above. Too often they and their children remain mired in long-term poverty.

Home care workers' economic plight is compounded by a legal bind. In most of the country, they are classified as independent contractors. Technically "self-employed," they have no outside employer (even though their pay often comes from federal or state funds like Medicaid). As a result, they get no employer-sponsored benefits or workers compensation insurance, and they are responsible for paying both the employee and employer portions of their payroll taxes out of their own paltry paychecks. Moreover, federal anti-trust law bans independent contractors from unionizing or bargaining collectively. In the eyes of the law, home care workers are not workers, but businesses (as self-employed individuals). Any effort to join together and unionize, therefore, is viewed as business "collusion."

This makes the recent west-coast union victories all the more remarkable. In California, Oregon, and Washington, organized labor in coalition with disabilities activists, senior citizens' lobbies and community groups forged a new three-step organizing strategy. In the process, they have transformed the structure of employment in the home-health care sector.

The strategy was born in a fifteen-year struggle in California. In-Home Supportive Services (IHSS), the state's massive home care program, is the nation's largest and currently employs more than 202,000 workers. The Service Employees International Union (SEIU) first attempted to organize IHSS workers in the 1980s. But state courts created a roadblock in 1987, ruling that home care workers were neither employees of the state of California (which paid them) nor employees of the county (to whom they submitted their semi-monthly time-sheets). Home health care worker Amanda Figueroa testified before the Los Angeles County Board of Supervisors in 2001 that the workers had been like "ping-pong balls" tossed between the state and county with neither willing to accept fiscal responsibility for wage increases or benefit coverage.

"The state and the counties didn't want to take responsibility for home care. We realized that a public authority was needed that could focus on developing a stable, professional workforce and improving the quality of care," said Tyrone Freeman, president of SEIU Local 434B. Following the court decision, SEIU developed the public authority strategy along with consumer advocates including the California

Senior Legislature, the California Foundation for Independent Living Centers, the Congress of California Seniors, and IHSS participants. United under the slogan of "Keep what works, fix what's wrong and fund it!!!" this coalition won passage of public authority legislation in 1992 which empowered counties to increase their local control of IHSS, established mechanisms for consumer input into policy, and created an "employer of record" for workers. This in effect established an employment relationship between home care workers and the public authority, enabling the SEIU to move forward with organizing drives.

Public authorities are commissions with powerful rights to oversee and manage local home health programs. Their advisory boards consist of a majority of IHSS consumers. The authorities set up registries of qualified workers to link long-term care consumers with home care workers. Some also operate specialized training programs.

> **Who Are Home Care Workers?**
>
> A recent U.S. General Accounting Office study found that over 90% of all home care workers in the nation are women, one-third are African American, nearly one-fifth are Hispanic and 20% are immigrants. The same report notes that one out of every four home care workers is unmarried with young children. Of 2 million paraprofessionals employed within the long-term care sector, 600,000 earn wages below the poverty line, according to the Service Employees International Union (SEIU).
>
> In California, 77% of IHSS home care workers are women; half are between the ages of 41 and 60; most work part time. Almost 40% are relatives paid to do care work for parents, spouses, and the like.

The public authority model spread throughout California, county by county, through the rest of the decade, and was reinforced in follow-up legislation in 1999. By the end of the 90s, seven counties with over 50% of California's IHSS home care workers developed public authorities: Alameda, Contra Costa, Los Angeles, Monterey, San Francisco, San Mateo, and Santa Clara. Stakeholders—workers, clients, and the new authorities—in these counties built statewide coalitions like the Public Interest Center on Long-Term Care and IHSS Agenda, whose dogged efforts kept public officials aware of the need for further improvements in the IHSS system. In 1999, SEIU Local 434B won the right to represent 74,000 home care workers in Los Angeles County. It was the biggest union victory in the state, in terms of numbers of new members, since the 1940s. That same year, the seven public authorities together with activists successfully advocated for additional legislation that mandated what had previously been optional: designating an employer of record for all IHSS workers and establishing consumer-majority advisory committees to oversee IHSS delivery issues. Faced with these requirements, 58 California counties have established public authorities.

The 1999 legislation also mandated that California pay 65% of the wages and benefits of home care workers above a minimum threshold, so that total compensation could increase gradually to $11.50 per hour over a four-year period (up from the minimum wage of $4.25 in 1991), if counties funded the remaining 35%. While organized labor spearheaded this effort, these benefits could have never been won without assistance from consumers and the public authorities.

Economist Candace Howes recently evaluated the impact of nearly doubling

IHSS workers' wages in San Francisco county. She found that IHSS jobs in the county represent 8% of all low-wage jobs, 16% of low-wage jobs available to women and 25% of all low-wage jobs available to immigrant women without English language proficiency. Her analysis suggests increasing wages for home care workers reduced San Francisco's overall poverty rate by approximately 16%.

Today, both the Service Employees International Union (SEIU) and American Federation of State, County and Municipal Employees (AFSCME) are working to replicate the public authority model in many states throughout the country.

Following the strategic steps pioneered in California, the unions first establish an employer-of-record for home care workers. Second, they organize and hold elections, and finally, they bargain with the authority for improvements in pay and working conditions.

Oregon voters approved a constitutional amendment on November 2000 creating a statewide quality home care commission modeled after California's IHSS public authority. This entity became the "employer of record" for 13,000 independent contractors who assist nearly 20,000 long-term care consumers. In December 2001, independent contractors who were previously prohibited from collective bargaining voted—92% in favor—to join SEIU Local 503. In June 2003, the state approved a contract with SEIU Local 503 that for the first time offered home care workers paid health insurance and worker compensation coverage while increasing their wages by $0.70 per hour and providing paid vacation for the first time in the program's history.

In November 2001, voters in Washington passed ballot initiative 775, approving a statewide home-care public authority to serve as the employer of record for 26,000 home care workers. "It was the first time ever that collective bargaining rights were extended through a ballot measure," the Washington State SEIU Local 503 organizing director told the Northwest Labor Press.

Eighty-four percent of Washington home care workers supported the call to unionize. But one lesson from the Washington case is that in the current state fiscal environment, unionization doesn't always mean better pay. In Washington, any agreement by the public authority board must be approved by the legislature and the governor. The legislature passed a raise for the home health care workers, only to see it vetoed by Democratic Gov. Gary Locke in the name of a balanced budget.

Still, the unionized public authority model has clearly brought gains. By serving as the employer of record for individuals previously considered independent contractors, the public authorities in California, Oregon, and Washington allowed almost 300,000 home care workers in California to collectively bargain for higher compensation and other changes. While for some, the financial gains have been small, for many others, pay increased dramatically.

Moreover, the election victories represent an area of growth for the labor movement. David Rolf, an organizer of the Los Angeles County union drive, told the *New York Times*, "It is a campaign where we reached out to low-income, women workers, workers of color and immigrant workers. If you look at the demographic changes in Southern California, the labor movement has to figure out how to bring these workers in because they are the backbone of the new, low-wage service-sector economy."

Twelve million people need long-term care services and support. As the baby-boomers age, the numbers will skyrocket. As researcher Janet Heinritz-Canterbury puts it, "The SEIU elections represented major headway not only for homecare workers on the west coast but for homecare consumers, and for society in general, which will benefit from a more stable workforce able to provide the services that will be increasingly needed over the next twenty years."

Stu Schneider, Special Projects Associate for the Paraprofessional Healthcare Institute (PHI), provides assistance in business development and public contract procurement to home care cooperatives.

RESOURCES: "Collaborating to Improve In-Home Supportive Services," Janet Heinritz-Canterbury, Paraprofessional Healthcare Institute (2002); "13,000 Home Care Workers in Oregon Vote Overwhelmingly to Join SEIU," Labor Research Association <www.laborresearch.org> (January 8, 2002).

Article 19
PRICING THE PRICELESS
Inside the Strange World of Cost-Benefit Analysis
LISA HEINZERLING AND FRANK ACKERMAN
March/April 2003

How strictly should we regulate arsenic in drinking water? Or carbon dioxide in the atmosphere? Or pesticides in our food? Or oil drilling in scenic places? The list of environmental harms and potential regulatory remedies often appears to be endless. In evaluating a proposed new initiative, how do we know if it is worth doing or not? Is there an objective way to decide how to proceed? Cost-benefit analysis promises to provide the solution—to add up the benefits of a public policy and compare them to the costs.

The costs of protecting health and the environment through pollution control devices and other approaches are, by their very nature, measured in dollars. The other side of the balance, calculating the benefits of life, health, and nature in dollars and cents, is far more problematic. Since there are no natural prices for a healthy environment, cost-benefit analysis creates artificial ones. Researchers, for example, may ask a cross-section of the affected population how much they would pay to preserve or protect something that can't be bought in a store. The average American household is supposedly willing to pay $257 to prevent the extinction of bald eagles, $208 to protect humpback whales, and $80 to protect gray wolves.

Costs and benefits of a policy, however, frequently fall at different times. When the analysis spans a number of years, future costs and benefits are *discounted,* or treated as equivalent to smaller amounts of money in today's dollars. The case for discounting begins with the observation that money received today is worth a little more than money received in the future. (For example, if the interest rate is 3%, you only need to deposit about $97 today to get $100 next year. Economists would say that, at a *3% discount rate,* $100 next year has a *present value* of $97.) For longer periods of time, or higher discount rates, the effect is magnified. The important issue for environmental policy is whether this logic also applies to outcomes far in the future, and to opportunities—like long life and good health—that are not naturally stated in dollar terms.

Why Cost-Benefit Analysis Doesn't Work

The case for cost-benefit analysis of environmental protection is, at best, wildly optimistic and, at worst, demonstrably wrong. The method simply does not offer the policy-making panacea its adherents promise. In practice, cost-benefit analysis frequently produces false and misleading results. Moreover, there is no quick fix, because these failures are intrinsic to the methodology, appearing whenever it is applied to any complex environmental problem.

It puts dollar figures on values that are not commodities, and have no price.
Artificial prices have been estimated for many benefits of environmental regulation. Preventing retardation due to childhood lead poisoning comes in at about $9,000 per lost IQ point. Saving a life is ostensibly worth $6.3 million. But what can it mean to say that one life is worth $6.3 million? You cannot buy the right to kill someone for $6.3 million, nor for any other price. If analysts calculated the value of life itself by asking people what it is worth to them (the most common method of valuation of other environmental benefits), the answer would be infinite. The standard response is that a value like $6.3 million is not actually a price on an individual's life or death. Rather, it is a way of expressing the value of small risks of death. If people are willing to pay $6.30 to avoid a one in a million increase in the risk of death, then the "value of a statistical life" is $6.3 million.

It ignores the collective choice presented to society by most public health and environmental problems.
Under the cost-benefit approach, valuation of environmental benefits is based on individuals' private decisions as consumers or workers, not on their public values as citizens. However, policies that protect the environment are often public goods, and are not available for purchase in individual portions. In a classic example of this distinction, the philosopher Mark Sagoff found that his students, in their role as citizens, opposed commercial ski development in a nearby wilderness area, but, in their role as consumers, would plan to go skiing there if the development was built. There is no contradiction between these two views: as individual consumers, the students would have no way to express their collective preference for wilderness preservation. Their individual willingness to pay for skiing would send a misleading signal about their views as citizens.

It is often impossible to arrive at a meaningful social valuation by adding up the willingness to pay expressed by individuals. What could it mean to ask how much you personally are willing to pay to clean up a major oil spill? If no one else contributes, the clean-up won't happen regardless of your decision. As the Nobel Prize-winning economist Amartya Sen has pointed out, if your willingness to pay for a large-scale public initiative is independent of what others are paying, then you probably have not understood the nature of the problem.

It systematically downgrades the importance of the future.

One of the great triumphs of environmental law is that it seeks to avert harms to people and to natural resources in the future, and not only within this generation, but in future generations as well. Indeed, one of the primary objectives of the National Environmental Policy Act, which has been called our basic charter of environmental protection, is to nudge the nation into "fulfill[ing] the responsibilities of

---

The Use and Misuse of Cost-Benefit Analysis:
Arsenic in Drinking Water

One thing is certain: arsenic is bad for you. It causes cancers of the bladder, lungs, skin, kidneys, nasal passages, liver, and prostate, as well as other cardiovascular, pulmonary, neurological, immunological, and endocrine problems. It is found naturally in rock formations and dissolves into drinking water supplies, the principal source of exposure.

Starting in 1942, federal law set the standard limiting arsenic in drinking water to 50 parts per billion (ppb). In 1962, the U.S. Public Health Service recommended that drinking water should not contain more than 10 ppb. In January 2001, EPA finally adopted this standard (recommended by the World Health Organization and adopted by many European countries). Less than two months later, the Bush administration withdrew the new rule—only to accept it again after eight months of further review and debate.

In developing the new standard, EPA considered four possible standards: 3, 5, 10, and 20 ppb. On the cost side, detailed engineering descriptions are available for an array of possible technologies for water treatment and disposal of resulting residues. EPA's estimates express only a narrow range of uncertainty about costs. If the chosen pollution control technologies become cheaper once the arsenic rule is implemented—as often happens when environmental rules are enforced—the cost estimates will prove too high.

On the benefit side, reduction in arsenic in drinking water has many health advantages. However, EPA's analysts were only able to produce quantitative estimates of the health effects for bladder and lung cancer; all numerical analysis of benefits refers to preventing these two cancers alone. EPA set the value of an avoided death at $6.1 million in 1999 dollars, based on "wage-risk" studies measuring the wage premium required to attract workers to dangerous jobs. For other health effects, EPA found that there was no "willingness-to-pay" value available for nonfatal cancers—so it used the value of reducing chronic bronchitis instead! EPA did not provide a dollar equivalent at all for health effects other than bladder and lung cancers.

The range between the upper and lower estimates of health benefits reflects solely the uncertainty about the number of avoided cancers. Costs and monetized benefits are roughly comparable for 20 ppb and 10 ppb. At 5 ppb and 3 ppb, the monetized benefits are below the costs.

AEI-Brookings Analysis

The AEI-Brookings Joint Center for Regulatory Studies has been a vocal proponent of cost-benefit analysis of environmental rules. Nevertheless, when EPA first issued its new arsenic rule, AEI-Brookings produced a highly critical study authored by Robert Hahn and Jason Burnett. EPA had erred in two ways, the AEI-Brookings study concluded, which led

each generation as trustee of the environment for succeeding generations."

The time periods involved in protecting the environment are often enormous—even many centuries, in such cases as climate change, radioactive waste, etc. With time spans this long, any discounting will make even global catastrophes seem trivial. At a discount rate of 5%, for example, the deaths of a billion people 500 years from now become less serious than the death of one person today. Seen in this way, discounting looks like a fancy justification for foisting our problems off onto the people who come after us.

It ignores considerations of distribution and fairness.
Cost-benefit analysis adds up all the costs of a policy, adds up all the benefits,

---

to overestimates of the benefits of arsenic reduction.

First, the study criticized EPA for failing to discount the lives saved by the arsenic rule. Because exposure to arsenic leads to cancer only after a latency period, Hahn and Burnett thought EPA should have discounted the benefits of the rule. Without citing any arsenic-related scientific evidence, Hahn and Burnett picked a latency period of 30 years as their "best estimate." This guess, combined with a 7 percent discount rate, had the effect of reducing the present value of a life saved from $6.1 million to $1.1 million.

Second, the AEI-Brookings study criticized EPA for assuming that the number of cancer cases due to arsenic is proportional to total exposure. Making up a different relationship between exposure and cancer, Hahn and Burnett, neither of whom is a scientist, guessed that there were only one-fifth as many cases of cancer due to arsenic as EPA had projected. With these and other adjustments, Hahn and Burnett found the costs of arsenic reduction to be roughly ten times the benefits, costing a shocking $65 million per life saved. They speculated that even 50 ppb might be too strict a standard, in light of the low benefits.

When the National Academy of Sciences (NAS) reviewed the arsenic standard yet again, in 2001, it found exactly the opposite of Hahn and Burnett's "best estimate." That is, NAS concluded that arsenic would cause more cancer cases than EPA had projected. This finding, no doubt combined with the public outcry over the issue, helped persuade the Bush administration to relent and accept the 10 ppb standard.

Public Debate

Once the rival EPA and Hahn-Burnett numbers made their way into the public forum, the assumptions, qualifications, and uncertainties surrounding them were forgotten.

The Washington Post, for example, ran a series of opinion pieces criticizing EPA's 10 ppb standard when originally issued in early 2001. Because the rule was predicted to cost $210 billion and the benefits were valued at $170 billion, these essays concluded that the rule was not worth it. They completely ignored the many unquantified benefits EPA had felt certain would flow from the rule.

The articles also referred to the Hahn-Burnett analysis without even mentioning the discounting and the dubious estimates that so influenced its results. Journalist Michael Kinsley noted the $65 million price tag per life saved according to Hahn and Burnett's analysis, and opined, without dwelling on the details, that its assumptions seemed "reasonable."

The public dialogue in the aftermath of the Bush administration's initial withdrawal of the new arsenic rule was not about discounting future life-saving, or cancer risk assessment, or the value of a life. Yet the numerical estimates of the benefits turn almost entirely on these issues, and the theories on which they rest. Cost-benefit analysis has not enriched the public dialogue; it has impoverished it, covering the topic with poorly understood numbers rather than clarifying the underlying clash of values.

and compares the totals. Implicit in this innocuous-sounding procedure is the assumption that it doesn't matter who gets the benefits and who pays the costs. Yet isn't there an important difference between spending state tax revenues, say, to improve the parks in rich communities, and spending the same revenues to clean up pollution in poor communities?

The problem of equity runs even deeper. Benefits are typically measured by willingness to pay for environmental improvement, and the rich are able and willing to pay for more than the poor. Imagine a cost-benefit analysis of locating an undesirable facility, such as a landfill or incinerator. Wealthy communities are willing to pay more for the benefit of not having the facility in their backyards; thus, under the logic of cost-benefit analysis, the net benefits to society will be maximized by putting the facility in a low-income area. In reality, pollution is typically dumped on the poor without waiting for formal analysis. Still, cost-benefit analysis rationalizes and reinforces the problem, allowing environmental burdens to flow downhill along the income slopes of an unequal society.

Should We Laugh—or Cry?

When it comes to cost-benefit analysis, nothing is out of bounds: everything has a price, and no inference is too heartless for the "hard science" of economics. The following stories are not the work of a lunatic fringe, but on the contrary, reflect how some of the most influential and well-known cost-benefit practitioners view the world.

Several years ago, states were suing tobacco companies for medical expenditures resulting from cigarette smoking. At that time, W. Kip Viscusi, a professor of law and economics at Harvard, concluded that states, in fact, saved money as the result of smoking by their citizens. Why? Because they died early, saving the states expenses on nursing home care and other services associated with an aging population! Viscusi even suggested that "cigarette smoking should be subsidized rather than taxed."

Take the problem of lead poisoning in children. One of the most serious and disturbing effects of lead is the neurological damage it can cause in young children, including permanently lowered mental ability. Randall Lutter, a researcher at the AEI-Brookings Joint Center for Regulatory Studies, put a dollar figure on the damage by looking at how much parents spent on a treatment designed to cause excretion of lead from the body. Parental spending on this treatment, according to Lutter, supports an estimate of $1,500 per IQ point lost due to lead poisoning. Previous economic analyses by EPA, based on the decrease in the children's expected future earnings, have estimated the value to be much higher—up to $9,000 per IQ point. Based on his lower figure, Lutter suggest that "agencies should consider relaxing their lead standards."

For sheer analytical audacity, Lutter's study faces some stiff competition from another study concerning children. Here, researchers examined mothers' car-seat fastening practices. They calculated the difference between the time required to fasten the seats correctly and the time mothers actually spent fastening their children into their seats. Then they assigned a monetary value to this interval of time based on the mothers' hourly wage rate (or, in the case of non-working moms, based on a guess at the wages they might have earned). When mothers saved time—and, by hypothesis, money—by fastening their children's car seats incorrectly, they were, according to the researchers, implicitly placing a finite monetary value on the life-threatening risks to their children posed by car accidents. Building on this calculation, the researchers were able to answer the vexing question of how much a statistical child's life is worth to her mother: $500,000.

Conclusion

There is nothing objective about the basic premises of cost-benefit analysis. Treating individuals solely as consumers, rather than as citizens with a sense of moral responsibility, represents a distinct and highly questionable worldview. Likewise, discounting reflects judgments about the nature of environmental risks and citizens' responsibilities toward future generations.

These assumptions beg fundamental questions about ethics and equity, and one cannot decide whether to embrace them without thinking through the whole range of moral issues they raise. Yet once one has thought through these issues, there is no need then to collapse the complex moral inquiry into a series of numbers. Pricing the priceless just translates our inquiry into a different language, one with a painfully impoverished vocabulary.

Lisa Heinzerling is a professor of law at Georgetown University Law School, specializing in environmental law. Frank Ackerman is Director of Research and Policy at the Global Development and Environment Institute at Tufts University, and a founder of D&S.

This article is a condensed version of the report *Pricing the Priceless*, published by the Georgetown Environmental Law and Policy Institute at Georgetown University Law Center. The full report *Pricing the Priceless* is available on-line at <www. ase.tufts.edu/gdae/publications/C-B%20 pamphlet%20final.pdf>. Ackerman and Heinzerling's book on these and related issues, *Priceless: Human Health, the Environment, and the Limits of the Market*, will be published by The New Press in January 2004.

Article 20

DRUG PRICES IN CRISIS
The Case Against Protectionism

DEAN BAKER
May/June 2001

In recent years, drug prices have risen to astronomical levels. In the United States, senior citizens are increasingly unable to afford prescription medication, while in developing nations, life-saving drugs are being priced out of reach for tens of millions of people with AIDS. In both cases, there is a single explanation for soaring drug prices: patent protection. If the pharmaceutical industry's patent monopolies were eliminated, most drugs would sell for only a fraction of their current cost.

Remarkably, however, the issue of drug patent monopolies rarely arises in public debate. Patent protection is a form of protectionism, but that's problematic terminology in a political climate where support for "free trade" is considered the only respectable opinion. So the pharmaceutical industry has managed to frame patent protection as a matter of "intellectual property rights" instead. Rarely has an industry been so successful in controlling the language of debate.

The industry has had a lot of help from the economics profession. Mainstream economists have developed an extensive body of research on the expected consequences of protection or monopoly pricing. If they were really as committed to efficiency and free trade as they pretend to be, they would be screaming about drug patents at the top of their lungs. The reason they don't is that they hold the drug industry in much higher esteem than manufacturing workers who might benefit from other forms of protectionism.

Of course, patent protection for prescription drugs, like all forms of protectionism, does serve a purpose—to provide industry with an incentive to research new drugs. If any firm could produce and sell every new drug that was developed, then no company would ever have a reason to spend money on research. However, the fact that drug patents can provide an incentive for research does not mean that they are the only or best way to support research. In fact, most biomedical research is currently supported by the federal government or private foundations, charities, and universities—not undertaken by private companies in anticipation of future sales.

We can only assess the full costs of patent protection if we recognize it as a form of protectionism, and look for all of the distortions that economists would expect protectionism to create. Once we do that, we'll see that the benefits derived from state-sanctioned monopoly protection are not justified by the quality and quantity of research that the pharmaceutical industry undertakes.

The Economics of Protectionism

Patent monopolies are a windfall for the pharmaceutical industry. Under the present system, a single firm gets to control the sale of a drug for the duration of its patent. Evidence from countries without effective protection for patents, or for drug prices after patents expire, indicates that most drugs would only sell for 25% of their patent protected price. In some cases, the difference is much greater. For example, the current state-of-the-art combination of anti-viral AIDS drugs sells in the United States for approximately $10,000 a year, according to the pharmaceutical industry. By contrast, a leading Indian manufacturer of generic drugs believes that it can sell the same combination profitably for $350 per year.

Why the huge gap between the monopoly patent protected price and the competitive market price? Because most drugs are relatively cheap to produce. Drugs are expensive because the government gives the industry a monopoly, not because they cost a lot to manufacture.

The costs of patent protection to consumers are enormous. The industry, which includes such giants as GlaxoSmithKline, Pfizer, and Bristol-Myers Squibb, estimates that it sold $106 billion worth of drugs in 2000. If eliminating patent protection had reduced the price of these drugs by 75%, then consumers would have saved $79 billion. This figure, to put it in perspective, is 30% more than what the federal government spends on education each year. It's more than ten times the amount that the federal government spends on Head Start. And it roughly equals the nation's annual bill for foreign oil.

What do we get for this money? Last year, the pharmaceutical industry, according to its own figures, spent $22.5 billion on domestic drug research (and another $4 billion on research elsewhere). For tax purposes, the industry claimed research expenditures of just $16 billion. Since these expenditures qualify for a 20% tax credit, the federal government directly covered $3.2 billion of the industry's research spending (20% of the $16 billion reported on tax returns). Even if we accept the $22.5 billion figure as accurate, this still means that the industry, after deducting the government contribution, spent just over $19 billion of its own money on drug research.

In other words, consumers (and the government, through Medicaid and other programs) spent an extra $79 billion on drugs because of patent protection, in order to get the industry to spend $19 billion of its own money on research. This comes out to more than four dollars in additional spending on drugs for every dollar that the industry spent on research. The rest of the money went mainly to:

- Marketing—The industry spends tens of billions each year to convince us (or our doctors) that its new drugs are absolutely essential and completely harmless.
- Protecting patent monopolies—Pharmaceutical companies regularly stand near the top in contributing to political campaigns. It's no accident that so many politicians are willing to push their cause.
- Profits—The pharmaceutical industry consistently ranks at the top in return on investment. It pulled in more than $20 billion in profits for 1999.

If spending an extra four dollars on drugs in order to persuade the industry to spend one dollar on research doesn't sound like a good deal, don't worry. It gets worse.

The Inefficiencies of Protectionism

Mainstream economists, who usually love to recite the evils of government protection, have been mostly silent on the issue of patent protection for drugs. But the evils are visible for all to see.

One major source of waste is research spending on imitation or "copycat" drugs. When a company gets a big hit with a new drug like Viagra or Claritin, its competitors will try to patent comparable drugs in order to get a slice of the market. In a world with patent protection, this can be quite beneficial to consumers, since a second drug creates some market competition. However, in the absence of patent protection, the incentive for copycat research would be unnecessary, since anyone who wanted to produce Viagra or Claritin would be free to do so, thereby pushing prices down.

How much do drug companies spend on copycat research? The industry won't say. But the Food and Drug Administration (FDA), in evaluating "new" drugs, considers only one third of them to be qualitatively new or better than existing drugs, while classifying the other two thirds as comparable to existing drugs. This doesn't mean that two thirds of research spending goes to copycat drugs; after all, the breakthrough drugs probably require more research spending, on average, than copycats. But suppose the industry wasted just 20% of its $19 billion in research spending on copycat drugs. This would bring the value of that spending down to $15 billion. That means consumers and the government are paying more than five dollars on drugs for each dollar of useful research.

The evils of protectionism don't end there. Prescription drugs present a classic case of asymmetric information: The drug companies know more about their drugs than the doctors who prescribe them, and far more than the patients who take them. The lure of monopoly profits gives the industry an enormous incentive to overstate the benefits and understate the risks of the newest wonder drugs. A June 2000 New England Journal of Medicine study found that the media consistently offered glowing accounts of drug breakthroughs. According to the study, the main villains in distorting the news were the public- relations departments of the drug manufacturers.

Still more serious is evidence that published research findings may be influenced by the drug industry's support. Last summer, the New York Times cited data showing that drugs, when tested by researchers who were supported by the drug's manufacturer, were found to be significantly more effective than existing drugs 89% of the time. By contrast, drugs tested by neutral researchers were found to be significantly more effective only 61% of the time.

Even if the industry's research could be completely trusted, there is still another problem created by the patent system—secrecy. The industry generally maintains the right to control the dissemination of findings from the research it supports. In some cases, this can mean a delay of months or even years before a researcher can disclose her findings at a conference or in a journal. In April 1996, for example, the Wall Street Journal reported on a British drug company's efforts to suppress a study showing that Synthroid, a drug to control thyroid problems, was no more effective than much cheaper alternatives.

THE USES OF DRUG MONEY
Drug Company Revenues, Profits, and Spending, 1999

Company	Revenues	Profits (as % of revenue)	Mrktg Costs (as % of revenue)	R&D (as % of revenue)
Merck	$32,714,000	18.0%	15.9%	6.3%
Pfizer	$16,204,000	19.6%	39.2%	17.1%
Eli Lilly	$10,003,000	27.2%	27.6%	17.8%
Schering-Plough	$9,176,000	23.0%	37.4%	13.0%
Pharmacia & Upjohn	$7,253,000	11.1%	38.6%	19.8%

Source: Families USA

In other cases, the secrecy is even more extreme. When the industry funds studies designed to prove that drugs are safe and effective enough to win FDA approval, it routinely keeps the results secret as proprietary information. This research may contain important clues about how best to use the new drug, or even about other factors affecting patients' health. Generally, however, the scientific community will not have access to it.

By creating incentives to misrepresent, falsify, or conceal research findings, patent monopolies are harmful to our pocketbooks as well as our health. At the very least, consumers may waste money on new, patent-protected drugs that are no more effective than existing drugs whose patents have expired. For example, a recent study estimated that consumers were spending $6 billion a year on a patented medication for patients with heart disease, which was no more effective than generic alternatives in preventing heart problems. As a result of industry propaganda, consumers might also spend money on drugs that could be less effective than cheaper alternatives—or on drugs that could even be hazardous to their health.

Another byproduct of monopoly drug pricing—the underground market—also has detrimental effects. When drugs can be sold profitably at prices that are much lower than their patent protected prices, consumers may seek underground sources for drugs. The most obvious way to do this is to purchase drugs in countries that either impose price controls or don't have the same patent protection as the United States. In recent years, there has been a much-publicized flow of senior citizens to Canada and Mexico in search of lower cost drugs. In the case of people traveling to Canada, the major cost to consumers is the waste of their time. However, when people buy drugs in countries with less stringent safety regulations, the health consequences may be severe.

The Proven Alternative

Listing the problems associated with drug patents would be an empty intellectual exercise—unless there were alternative ways to support research. Fortunately, there are. The federal government currently supports $18 billion a year in biomedical research through the National Institutes of Health (NIH) and the Centers for Disease Control (CDC). (The vast majority of NIH-funded research is carried out at universities and research centers across the country; less than 20% is conducted on the campus of the Institutes themselves.) In addition, universities, private foundations, and charities fund a combined total of approximately $10 billion worth of research annually. Added together, these institutions spend 25% more on research than the pharmaceutical industry claims to spend, and nearly twice as much as the industry reports on tax returns.

Over the years, the research supported by government and non-profit institutions has led to numerous medical breakthroughs, including the discovery and development of penicillin and the polio vaccine. More recently, NIH-supported research has played a central role in developing AZT as an AIDS drug, and in developing Taxol, a leading cancer drug. The NIH's impressive list of accomplishments over the last five decades proves that the government can support effective research.

Traditionally, the NIH has focused on basic research and early phases of drug testing, while the pharmaceutical industry has engaged primarily in the later phases of drug testing—which include conducting clinical trials and carrying drugs through the FDA approval process. However, there is not a sharp division between the type of research done by the NIH and that undertaken by the pharmaceutical industry; the NIH has conducted research in all areas of drug development. There is no reason to believe that, given enough funding, the NIH could not effectively carry out all phases of drug research.

While the idea of a panel of government-supported scientists (most of whom would probably be affiliated with universities and other research institutions) deciding which drugs should be researched may seem scary, consider the current situation. Drug-company executives make their research decisions based on their assessment of a drug's profitability. In turn, that assessment depends on whether the company can get insurance companies to pay for the drug, whether it can effectively lobby legislators to have Medicaid and other government programs pay for it, and whether it can count on the courts to fully enforce its patents against competitors. It is these factors—not consideration of what will benefit the public's health—that dominate the industry's decisions about research. It is hard to believe that publicly accountable bodies that are charged with directing research for the general good would not produce better results.

The arithmetic behind a proposed switch is straightforward. If the federal government spent an additional $20 billion a year to support research at the NIH and various non-profit and educational institutions, it would more than fully replace the useful research conducted by the pharmaceutical industry. The cost to the federal government would be less than the cost of the prescription drug plan that Al Gore advocated in last year's presidential campaign. If patent protection for drugs were eliminated, consumers would save more than $79 billion a year. These savings would increase with each passing year, since spending on drugs is currently rising at more than twice the rate of inflation.

Even assuming that the United States continues to rely on patent protection to support drug research for the immediate future, interim steps can be taken. First, it will be important to sharply restrict the worst abuses of the patent system. At the top of the list, the U.S. government should not be working with the pharmaceutical industry to impose its patents on developing countries. This is especially important in the case of AIDS drugs, since patent protection in sub-Saharan Africa may effectively be sentencing tens of million of people to death. There should also be pressure to allow the importation of drugs from nations where they are sold at lower prices, or even better, the imposition of domestic price controls.

A second priority is to create a greater opening for alternative sources of research. There should be more support for the NIH to carry some of its research through to the actual testing and approval of new drugs. The patents for these drugs should then be placed in the public domain, so that the industry can compete to supply the drugs at the lowest cost. In addition to bringing immediate benefits to consumers, this would allow for a clear test of the patent system's value as a means of supporting research, as compared with direct public support.

Back in the Middle Ages, the guild system was established to protect the secrets of masters from their apprentices. If you tried to make and sell hats but didn't belong to the hatmakers' guild, you'd be subject to arrest. Patents (and their cousin, copyrights) come out of this tradition. While most medieval restrictions have long since been discarded, patents have managed to survive and are now deeply enmeshed in our economic system. Not all forms of patent protection cause the problems associated with drug patents; in some areas, such as industrial processes, it may be reasonable to keep patent protection intact. But the case of drug patents cries out for the free market that economists say they favor, to wipe this feudal relic away.

Dean Baker is co-director of the Center for Economic and Policy Research and author of the Economic Reporting Review, an on-line commentary on economic reporting in the New York Times and Washington Post.

RESOURCES: *Annals of Thoracic Surgery* (September 2000): 883-888; *Wall Street Journal*, April 25, 1996, p. A1; Pharmaceutical Research and Manufacturers of America, www.phrma.org.

Article 21
CAUSE OF DEATH: INEQUALITY
ALEJANDRO REUSS
May/June 2001

Inequality kills.

You won't see inequality on a medical chart or a coroner's report under "cause of death." You won't see it listed among the top killers in the United States each year. All too often, however, it is social inequality that lurks behind a more immediate cause of death, be it heart disease or diabetes, accidental injury or homicide. Few of the top causes of death are "equal opportunity killers." Instead, they tend to strike poor people more than rich people, the less educated more than the highly educated, people lower on the occupational ladder more than those higher up, or people of color more than white people.

Statistics on mortality and life expectancy do not provide a perfect map of social inequality. For example, the life expectancy for women in the United States is about six years longer than the life expectancy for men, despite the many ways in which women are subordinated to men. Take most indicators of socioeconomic status, however, and most causes of death, and it's a strong bet that you'll find illness and injury (or "morbidity") and mortality increasing as status decreases.

Men with less than 12 years of education are more than twice as likely to die of chronic diseases (e.g., heart disease), more than three times as likely to die as a result of injury, and nearly twice as likely to die of communicable diseases, compared to those with 13 or more years of education. Women with family incomes below

$10,000 are more than three times as likely to die of diabetes, compared to those with family incomes above $25,000. African-Americans are more likely than whites to die of heart disease; stroke; lung, colon, prostate, and breast cancer, as well as all cancers combined; liver disease; diabetes; AIDS; accidental injury; and homicide. In all, the lower you are in a social hierarchy, the worse your health and the shorter your life is likely to be.

The Poor in the United States Are Not Well Off By World Standards

You often hear it said that even poor people in rich countries like the United States are rich compared to ordinary people in poor countries. While that may be true when it comes to consumer goods like televisions or telephones, which are widely available even to poor people in the United States, it's completely wrong when it comes to health.

In a 1996 study published in the *New England Journal of Medicine*, University of Michigan researchers found that African-American females living to age 15 in Harlem had a 65% chance of surviving to age 65, about the same as women in India. Meanwhile, Harlem's African-American males had only a 37% chance of surviving to age 65, about the same as men in Angola or the Democratic Republic of Congo. Among both African-American men and women, infectious diseases and diseases of the circulatory system were the prime causes of high mortality.

It takes more income to achieve a given life expectancy in a rich country like the United States than it does to achieve the same life expectancy in a less affluent country. So the higher money income of a low-income person in the United States, compared to a middle-income person in a poor country, does not necessarily translate into a longer life span. The average income per person in African-American families, for example, is more than five times the per capita income of El Salvador. The life expectancy for African-American men in the United States, however, is only about 67 years, the same as the average life expectancy for men in El Salvador.

Access to Health Care Is Not the Only Problem

Nearly one sixth of the U.S. population lacks health insurance, including about 44% of poor people. A poor adult with a health problem is only half as likely to see a doctor as a high-income adult. Adults living in low-income areas are more than twice as likely to be hospitalized for a health problem that could have been effectively treated with timely outpatient care, compared with adults living in high-income areas. Obviously, lack of access to health care is a major health problem.

But so are environmental and occupational hazards; communicable diseases; homicide and firearm-related injuries; and smoking, alcohol consumption, lack of exercise, and other risk factors. These dangers all tend to affect lower-income people more than higher-income, less-educated people more than more-educated, and people of color more than whites. African-American children are more than twice as likely as white children to be hospitalized for asthma, which is linked to air pollution. Poor men are nearly six times as likely as high-income men to have elevated blood-lead levels, which reflect both residential and workplace environmental hazards. African-American men are more than seven times as likely to fall victim to homicide as white men; African-American women, more than four times as likely as white women. The less education someone has, the more likely they are to smoke or to drink heavily. The lower someone's income, the less likely they are to get regular exercise.

Michael Marmot, a pioneer in the study of social inequality and health, notes that so-called diseases of affluence—disorders, like heart disease, associated with high-calorie and high-fat diets, lack of physical activity, etc.—are most prevalent among the *least affluent* people in rich societies. While recognizing the role of such "behavioral" risk factors as smoking in producing poor health, he argues, "It is not sufficient…to ask what contribution smoking makes to generating the social gradient in ill health, but we must ask, why is there a social gradient in smoking?" What appear to be individual "lifestyle" decisions often reflect a broader *social* epidemiology.

Greater Income Inequality Goes Hand in Hand with Poorer Health

Numerous studies suggest that the more unequal the income distribution in a country, state, or city, the lower the life expectancies for people at all income levels. One study published in the *American Journal of Public Health*, for example, shows that U.S. metropolitan areas with low per capita incomes and low levels of income inequality have lower mortality rates than areas with high median incomes and high levels of income inequality. Meanwhile, for a given per capita income range, mortality rates always decline as inequality declines.

R.G. Wilkinson, perhaps the researcher most responsible for relating health outcomes to overall levels of inequality (rather than individual income levels), argues that greater income inequality causes worse health outcomes independent of its effects on poverty. Wilkinson and his associates suggest several explanations for this relationship. First, the bigger the income gap between rich and poor, the less inclined the well-off are to pay taxes for public services they either do not use or use in low proportion to the taxes they pay. Lower spending on public hospitals, schools, and other basic services does not affect wealthy people's life expectancies very much, but it affects poor people's life expectancies a great deal. Second, the bigger the income gap is, the lower the overall level of social cohesion will be. High levels of social cohesion are associated with good health outcomes for several reasons. For example, people in highly cohesive societies are more likely to be active in their communities, reducing social isolation, a known health risk factor.

Numerous researchers have criticized Wilkinson's conclusions, arguing that the real reason income inequality tends to be associated with worse health outcomes is that it is associated with higher rates of poverty. But even if they are right and income inequality causes worse health *simply by bringing about greater poverty*, it hardly makes for a defense of inequality. Poverty and inequality are like partners in crime. "[W]hether public policy focuses primarily on the elimination of poverty or on reduction in income disparity," argue Wilkinson critics Kevin Fiscella and Peter Franks, "neither goal is likely to be achieved in the absence of the other."

Differences in Status May Be Just as Important as Income Levels

Even after accounting for differences in income, education, and other factors, the life expectancy for African-Americans is less than that for whites. U.S. researchers are beginning to explore the relationship between high blood pressure among African-Americans and the racism of the surrounding society. African-Americans tend to suffer from high blood pressure, a risk factor for circulatory disease, more often than whites. Moreover, studies have found that, when confronted with racism, African-Americans suffer larger and longer-lasting increases in blood pressure than when faced with other stressful situations. Broader surveys relating blood pressure in African-Americans to perceived instances of racial discrimination have yielded complex results, depending on social class, gender, and other factors.

Stresses cascade down social hierarchies and accumulate among the least empowered. Even researchers focusing on social inequality and health, however, have been surprised by the large effects on mortality. Over 30 years ago, Michael Marmot and his associates undertook a landmark study, known as Whitehall I, of health among British civil servants. Since the civil servants shared many characteristics regardless of job classification—an office work environment, a high degree of job security, etc.—the researchers expected to find only modest health differences among them. To their surprise, the study revealed a sharp increase in mortality with each step down the job hierarchy—even from the highest grade to the second highest. Over ten years, employees in the lowest grade were three times as likely to die as those in the highest grade. One factor was that people in lower grades showed a higher incidence of many "lifestyle" risk factors, like smoking, poor diet, and lack of exercise. Even when the researchers controlled for such factors, however, more than half the mortality gap remained.

Marmot noted that people in the lower job grades were less likely to describe themselves as having "control over their working lives" or being "satisfied with their work situation," compared to those higher up. While people in higher job grades were more likely to report "having to work at a fast pace," lower-level civil servants were more likely to report feelings of hostility, the main stress-related risk factor for heart disease. Marmot concluded that "psycho-social" factors—the psychological costs of being lower in the hierarchy—played an important role in the unexplained mortality gap. Many of us have probably said to ourselves, after a trying day on the job, "They're killing me." Turns out it's not just a figure of speech. Inequality kills—and it starts at the bottom.

Alejandro Reuss is co-editor of Dollars & Sense.

RESOURCES: Lisa Berkman, "Social Inequalities and Health: Five Key Points for Policy-Makers to Know," February 5, 2001, Kennedy School of Government, Harvard University; *Health, United States, 1998, with Socioeconomic Status and Health Chartbook,* National Center for Health Statistics <www.cdc.gov/nchs>; Ichiro Kawachi, Bruce P. Kennedy, and Richard G. Wilkinson, eds., *The Society and Population Health Reader, Volume I: Income Inequality and Health,* 1999; Michael Marmot, "Social Differences in Mortality: The Whitehall Studies," *Adult Mortality in Developed Countries: From Description to Explanation,* Alan D. Lopez, Graziella Caselli, and

Tapani Valkonen, eds.,1995; Michael Marmot, "The Social Pattern of Health and Disease," *Health and Social Organization: Towards a Health Policy for the Twenty-First Century,* David Blane, Eric Brunner, and Richard Wilkinson, eds., 1996; Arline T. Geronimus, et al., "Excess Mortality Among Blacks and Whites in the United States," *The New England Journal of Medicine 335* (21), November 21, 1996; Nancy Krieger, Ph.D., and Stephen Sidney, M.D., "Racial Discrimination and Blood Pressure: The CARDIA Study of Young Black and White Adults," *American Journal of Public Health* 86 (10), October 1996; *Human Development Report 2000,* UN Development Programme; *World Development Indicators 2000,* World Bank.

Article 22
THE SOCIAL RELATIONS OF HEALTH AND DISEASE
JEANNE WINNER
May/June 2001

In 1980, when the World Health Organization proclaimed that the planet was free of smallpox, it confirmed modern medicine's program for achieving health: Identify the microorganisms responsible for diseases, and then find a way to kill them without killing their human hosts. The announcement capped a century of spectacular achievements, including the discovery of antitoxins against diphtheria and syphilis, and the development of penicillin and other antibiotics. The eradication of smallpox supported the practicing faith of the medical profession: That scientific knowledge could promote human health by ending the tyranny of harmful microbes.

Forty years ago, French biologist René Dubos questioned this view. Health, he wrote, was not simply the absence of disease. Rather, it depended on human beings' "adapt[ing] to the total environment, which is constantly changing." The total environment includes not only our own physical state but also the quality of air, land, and water; our psychological condition; and our social relations with each other. Human activity is a major contributor to changes in the total environment. In recent years, tuberculosis, malaria, and cholera, which were in sharp decline, have returned, while new and frightening diseases like AIDS, Ebola virus, and toxic shock syndrome have appeared. In order to understand the resurgence of these and other health problems, we need to understand how we affect the total environment and how it affects us.

Food First

Medical practice implies that you can be healthy as long as you take the right antitoxins. But the social history of health suggests that nutrition, not medicine, has been the most important factor in eliminating infectious disease.

In 19th-century England, infectious diseases, especially respiratory diseases—tuberculosis, diphtheria, bronchitis, and pneumonia—were the principal causes of death. Smallpox had also been a leading killer. But by the early 1850s, all British citizens were required to take the smallpox vaccine. After that, the death rate from smallpox declined rapidly. However, death rates from other respiratory diseases also fell dramatically, even though there was no treatment or cure. For example, by the early 20th century, the death rate from tuberculosis had dropped by 90%, but doctors did not have an effective treatment for it until 1947.

Why were fewer people dying from respiratory diseases, with or without a cure? The most plausible explanation, according to population geneticist Richard Lewontin and others, is improved nutrition. A human being cannot contract tuberculosis without being exposed to the tubercle bacillus. But exposure does not guarantee sickness. People are more likely to contract the disease if they are poorly nourished and their immune systems are weak. In 19th-century England, where the majority of people were poor and poorly nourished, social relations were at least as important as microbes in helping to spread the disease. As the poorer classes began to eat better, their resistance to tuberculosis rose.

Consider the change in women's mortality rates. Today, British women live longer than men, but in the 19th century, they died earlier than men. The common explanation is that women died in childbirth until doctors began using antiseptic techniques to deliver babies. But death records show that 19th-century British women were dying more often of tuberculosis than of complications from childbirth. The popular analysis implied that medicine rescued women from the burden of dying from childbirth, that their female bodies and medical techniques were the problem. But as Lewontin has pointed out, social and economic changes—greater productivity in agriculture and industry, and higher wages—benefited women far more. These changes rescued women from the burden of grossly inferior nourishment, which made them vulnerable to dying young from tuberculosis.

Measles offers another example. Measles is a childhood disease with a completely different character depending on how well nourished the child is. In 19th-century England and the United States, measles killed children. In the 20th century, it has been a mild disease for most children in these countries. In Africa, however, measles is still killing children. Why? Because children in Africa are poor and poorly nourished, like most children in 19th-century England and the United States. The lack of nutrition reflects social relations—widespread poverty, poor living conditions, and a very unequal distribution of the necessities of life.

Corporate Control and Environmental Health

In the United States, significant numbers of people live in poverty and suffer from hunger, in spite of the enormous productivity of U.S. industry and agriculture. Similarly, modern industry and agriculture have chosen to produce under conditions that are extremely hazardous to their employees and often to consumers. These are social decisions—not made with popular consent—that affect the health of many.

In 1980, the White House Council on Environment Quality, after reviewing studies documenting the increase in the number of cancer patients between 1973 and 1976, concluded that the numbers would keep on rising. "Only a small portion of chemical carcinogens have been regulated to date," the Council said, "and…exposures to unregulated carcinogens will probably cause the incidence of cancer to continue to rise."

Since then, conditions have grown worse. The Environmental Protection Agency reports that U.S. industries now dump more than seven billion pounds of toxins into the environment each year. Some places are more seriously affected than others. In Louisiana, in an area stretching from Baton Rouge to just south of New Orleans, there are seven oil refineries and 150 heavy industrial plants operating along the Mississippi River. These facilities produced enormous amounts of toxic waste, which contains contaminants that cause cancer; harm infant and child development; injure the reproductive system; and may also damage the liver, skin, and kidneys, as well as the endocrine, neurological, and immune systems. Among residents of the area, known as "Cancer Alley," rates of cancer and other ailments are higher than the national average. But the state of Louisiana, in its eagerness to placate industry, does little to regulate industrial pollution. The sickness in "Cancer Alley" is due not just to pollutants but also to the political and economic relations that pit health against profits.

With the rise of commercial agriculture and agribusiness, farmers have vastly increased their use of pesticides, with devastating results. Richard Levins and Cynthia Lopez of the Harvard School of Public Health cite researchers who found that farmers in Kansas are more likely to contract cancer than other residents of the state. The farmers are significantly more likely to die of non-Hodgkin's lymphoma, leukemia, and cancers of the prostate and brain.

The Socioeconomics of Health

There is evidence that our place in the social hierarchy affects our health as well. Health depends on more than just meeting our physical needs. Social inequality also matters. Does aspirin help to ward off heart attacks? When researchers tried to test this hypothesis using male physicians, they couldn't measure the benefits, because the physicians, as a group, were so much healthier than the rest of the population: Their overall rate of fatal heart attacks was just 12% of the rate for men in general. Do you want to understand the correlation between secondary smoke and asthma in children? Medical research indicates that poverty alone is associated with asthma. So unless you control for socioeconomic status, you can't fully interpret the clinical results. Are you interested in predicting the likelihood of coronary disease? Be sure to look at class position, because it's a better predictor than cholesterol level. The lower a person's class, reports Richard Levins, the more likely the presence of coronary disease.

Even physiological reactions are related to class. In a series of Harvard studies, researchers found that upper-class and working-class adolescents responded differently to stress, even though they were doing equally well academically. Both groups of students responded to stress with a sudden increase in the level of cortisol, a hormone that the adrenal gland secretes after it releases adrenaline. But in the upper-class students, the cortisol level dropped quickly, while in the working-class students, it remained high. (A sustained high level of cortisol diverts energy from the growth, digestive, reproductive, and immune systems.) The upper-class students, in other words, had an upper-class physiology, and the working-class students, a working-class physiology.

Low-level, stressful jobs are also bad for your health. Between 1992 and 1996, researcher Ichiro Kawachi and his colleagues at the Harvard School of Public Health studied more than 21,000 women workers. They found that "women in poor jobs with high work demands, low levels of job control and little workplace social support are more likely to suffer poor health—and see their health decline—than are women in more flexible jobs with reasonable demands and social support."

Of course, socioeconomic status is not only a matter of class. In the United States, black people's average life span is ten years shorter than that of white people. The health of people of color is poorer than that of whites, even when they are well to do. Admittedly, these results may not just reflect social stress; as many studies indicate, racial discrimination extends to the provision of medical care. But having a high income is clearly not enough to protect oneself against the social stress of racial discrimination.

A Call for Healthy Social Relations

These findings throw into sharp relief the limitations of conventional medicine. Certainly microbes and molecules are important factors in health and disease. And certainly vaccines, medicines, and surgical interventions are valuable, in many cases. But health also depends on social conditions and our economic relationships with each other. Whether people have access to a healthy and abundant diet depends on wage levels, food distribution, and the agricultural system. Whether women and children are as well nourished as men depends on social relations and custom. Whether we are healthy also depends on characteristics that are harder to measure, such as social status, workplace relations, and discrimination.

How can we turn what we know about health into a program for better health for all? Organizing for higher wages builds health. Making sure the hungry are better fed builds health. The federal WIC (Women, Infants, and Children) program provides nutritious food to low-income women and their children up to age five. Its greatest weakness is its meager budget and limited scope. It is worth campaigning to expand both.

There are also grassroots campaigns that promote health. For example, the Blue Ridge Environmental Defense League (BREDL) has more than 50 chapters in North and South Carolina, Virginia, and Tennessee. BREDL activists have been organizing in local communities to stop landfill expansion, high and low-level nuclear dumps, corporate hog farms, four-lane highways, and clear-cut logging in national forests. In the Midwest, farmers are trying to block the advance of agribusiness. And in the Northwest, environmental groups have joined with labor unions to protect the environment and save jobs.

A healthy population requires a healthy society. If we want to be healthy, we can't just go to the doctor and take a pill. Instead, we need to live in a democratic society characterized by good working conditions; access to health care, housing, and food; greater income equality; and control over our lives.

Jeanne Winner is a member of the Dollars & Sense *collective.*

RESOURCES: Norman Daniels, Bruce Kennedy, and Ichiro Kawachi, eds., *Is Inequality Bad for Our Health?* (Beacon Press, 2000); René Dubos, *Mirage of Health: Utopias, Progress and Biological Change* (Harper, 1959); Nancy Krieger, "Refiguring 'Race': Epidemiology, Racialized Biology, and Biological Expressions of Race Relations," *International Journal of Health Services* 30 (1), 2000: 211-216; Richard Levins, "Is Capitalism a Disease?" *Monthly Review*, September 2000: 8-33; R Levins and C. Lopez, "Toward an Ecosocial View of Health." *International Journal of Health Services* 29 (2), 1999: 261-293; Richard Lewontin. *Biology as Ideology* (Harper Collins, 1993); Thomas McKown, *The Role of Medicine: Dream, Mirage, or Nemesis?* (Princeton University Press, 1979); Vicente Navarro, *Crisis, Health, and Medicine: A Social Critique* (Tavistock Publications, 1986); Richard G. Wilkinson, "Income Inequality, Social Cohesion, and Health: Clarifying the Theory—A Reply to Muntaner and Lynch," *International Journal of Health Services*, 29 (3), 1999: 525-543.

Article 23

"RAISE THE ALARM LOUDLY"
Africa confronts the AIDS epidemic.

AKIN JIMOH
May/June 2001

We were both standing on the sidewalk, watching the convoy of returning soldiers on their way to the military hospital in Victoria Island, Lagos, Nigeria. Amid the noise from the heavy-duty military vehicles and downtown traffic, my companion, Mohammed Farouk Auwalu, a former soldier in the Nigerian army, shook his head and muttered, "Many of them will most likely die soon or be out of the army like me with little or nothing to show for it. A lot of people don't know that many have died, others are dying, and many are walking in the shadow of death."

The convoy was returning from one of Nigeria's many peacekeeping missions elsewhere on the continent, but African wars were far from Auwalu's mind. He was talking about the specter of AIDS. In his mid-thirties and married, Auwalu is now retired, not because he cannot perform his assigned duties, but because he is living with HIV. He currently heads the Nigeria AIDS Alliance, an awareness group formed by people living with HIV/AIDS.

The Pandemic

So far, AIDS has killed 17 million Africans. It has orphaned about 12 million children. And about 25.3 million Africans (about 9% of the continent's total population) now live, like Auwalu, with HIV. According to the World Bank, the HIV infection rate in pregnant women in Blantyre, Malawi, increased from less than 5%

in 1985 to over 30% in 1997. In Francistown, Botswana, the rate climbed from less than 10% in 1991 to 43% in 1997. New figures from the United Nations Joint AIDS Program (UNAIDS) show that 3.8 million people in sub-Saharan Africa became infected with HIV during 2000. Meanwhile, 2.4 million Africans died of AIDS that year.

From the Horn of Africa to the Cape of Good Hope, HIV/AIDS is crippling national economies. Many African countries now face the enormous costs of fighting the epidemic and caring for the millions orphaned by AIDS, even as the most productive generation is decimated by the disease. A study published in the South African Journal of Economics in July 2000 concluded that, as a result of HIV/AIDS, South Africa's national income would be 17% lower in 2010 than it would have been otherwise. Overall, the World Bank estimates that HIV/AIDS has cut economic growth in Africa by about two-thirds.

"The AIDS situation in Africa is catastrophic and sub-Saharan Africa continues to head the list as the world's most affected region," says Dr. Peter Piot, executive director of UNAIDS. "One of the greatest causes for concern is that over the next few years, the epidemic is bound to get worse before it gets better." AIDS has struck virtually all sectors of society. Families have been devastated; husbands, wives, brothers, and sisters are dead or dying. Women, young people, and children are among the hardest hit.

How did it get this bad?

- *Migrant labor.* The prevalence of migrant labor in Southern Africa has greatly contributed to the high infection rates in Botswana, South Africa, Malawi, Namibia, Zambia, and Zimbabwe. As migrant laborers move from one work site to another, leaving their families behind, many engage in multiple sexual relationships.

- *Low social status of women.* Women account for half of Africa's HIV-positive population, according to the UN, and the infection rate for women is on the rise. Data from several African countries show infection rates for teenage girls five to six times the rates for teenage boys. Poverty forces many girls and women to trade their bodies for money. Meanwhile, the low social and economic status of women, argues UN Secretary General Kofi Annan, results in a "weaker ability to negotiate safe sex."

- *Lack of open discussion.* Cultural and religious inhibitions on the discussion of sex-related issues hindered AIDS prevention at an early stage. Repression against the media also inhibited the flow of information. At an HIV/AIDS meeting in Mexico in 1988, U.S. journalist and science writer Laurie Garrett saluted by name a Kenyan journalist who had broadcast AIDS information over an independent radio station. He was arrested within hours. The Zimbabwean and South African governments have also routinely targeted journalists disseminating information about AIDS.

- *Lack of quick government action.* Olikoye Ransome-Kuti, a pediatrician and former health minister of Nigeria, says that, even in the mid 1990s, the Nigerian military regime allocated a mere $3,000 annually to AIDS control programs. Now, 5.4% of Nigerians between the ages of 15 and 49—about 2.6 million people—live with HIV/AIDS. In many African countries, political turmoil and war contributed to a delayed government response.

- *Weak health-care systems.* In the mid 1980s, most African countries achieved child-immunization rates, to take just one indicator of basic public-health provision, of over 80%. In the following decade, rates fell below 20% in many African countries. Lack of access to basic health services has increased the rate of non-sexual (mother-to-child) HIV transmission.

- *Economic austerity programs.* The AIDS epidemic began its full onslaught in the mid-to-late 1980s, when the International Monetary Fund imposed structural adjustment programs (SAPs) on many African countries. Under the SAPs, national currencies were devalued and subsidies to critical sectors of the economy discontinued. With minimal funds available to governments, social infrastructure and services, including health services, suffered. Keith Hansen, deputy head of the World Bank's AIDS Campaign Team for Africa, admitted that SAPs had weakened African economies. Austerity has deprived African countries of the means to fight the epidemic.

- *The high cost of drugs.* Pharmaceutical companies like Bristol-Myers Squibb of the United States, GlaxoSmithKline of Great Britain, and Boerhinger Ingelheim GMBH of Germany sell their patented AIDS drugs for $10,000-15,000 per patient per year, three to five times the per capita income of South Africa (the highest in Africa).

Uganda, the place where AIDS first struck in Africa, now offers a model for combating the epidemic. The Ugandan government has helped bring about a mini-sexual revolution. In the mid 1980s, it began prevention campaigns on HIV/AIDS and other sexually transmitted diseases, and started promoting sex education generally. President Yoweri Museveni personally championed the AIDS-control program. Meanwhile, some debt relief and the creation of an anti-poverty program has resulted in a revival of the health system.

"When a lion comes to your village you must raise the alarm loudly," Museveni says. "This is what we did in Uganda; we took it seriously and achieved good results. AIDS...is not like smallpox or Ebola. AIDS can be prevented as it is transmitted through a few known ways. If we raise awareness sufficiently, it will stop." Between 1997 and 2000, while the HIV infection rate climbed from about 13% to nearly 20% in South Africa and from about 25% to over 35% in Botswana, it has actually decreased in Uganda, from 9.5% to 8.3%. Since there is no cure for AIDS, lower infection rates reflect the deaths of some people who already had AIDS—but also a lower rate of new HIV infections.

The Patents War

In Pretoria, South Africa, this past March, thousands of AIDS activists and HIV-positive youths descended on the country's High Court and the U.S. Embassy. Wearing "HIV-positive" T-shirts and baseball caps, hands locked together in solidarity, they marched in angry protest against the high cost of AIDS drugs. Their placards expressed their rage: "Lives Before Profits" and "AIDS Profiteer Deadlier Than The Virus." The battle over AIDS-drug patents had begun.

A new cocktail of generic AIDS drugs developed by the Indian drug company CIPLA threatens the big drug companies' lucrative monopolies. CIPLA has offered the drug at a cost of $350 per year per patient to the humanitarian organization Doctors Without Borders, and $600 per year per patient to African governments. In March, thirty-nine of the big pharmaceutical companies went to court to challenge the South African government's go-ahead on the sale of generic AIDS drugs, provoking the March protests.

A few weeks after the court battle began, Doctors Without Borders approached Yale University to convince it to release its patent on the AIDS drug dT4. Two Yale professors had developed dT4, which the university then licensed to Bristol-Myers Squibb. Professor William Prusoff, one of the developers, wrote during the height of the controversy that the drug should be either free or very inexpensive in sub-Saharan Africa, and expressed disappointment that it was not reaching the millions of people who desperately needed it. Not long after, Bristol-Myers announced that it would reduce the cost of d4T by 15% in the United States and 85% in the rest of the world, and that it would offer the drug for 15 cents per daily dose in the most afflicted areas of Africa. The other two pharmaceutical giants, GlaxoSmithKline and Boerhinger Ingelheim GMBH, are also expected to cut their AIDS-drug prices. The companies, however, remain steadfast about keeping their patent rights, which would leave ultimate control over prices and availability in their hands.

In response, the AIDS-devastated countries of Africa may resort to "compulsory licensing," ignoring the patents and proceeding with generic drugs. International convention recognizes the right of countries in states of national emergency to obtain or manufacture generic drugs, even in breach of drug-company patents. So far, President Thabo Mbeki of South Africa has resisted an official declaration of national emergency, though he promises to go forward with generic drugs. The U.S. government, under both former President Bill Clinton and current President George W. Bush, has promised not to challenge laws passed by African countries to improve access to AIDS drugs, even if U.S. patent laws are broken. It has not, however, pressed U.S. pharmaceutical firms to renounce their patent rights—which is why protestors targeted the U.S. embassy.

The battle is far from over. Even at 15 cents per day, or about $55 per year, AIDS drugs will remain beyond the means of most Africans. At the 8th Conference on Retroviruses and Opportunistic Infections in February 2001, doctors, scientists, and policymakers proposed that rich nations pay for drugs and other means to combat AIDS in Africa, with the United States paying $3 billion. Harvard economist Jeffrey Sachs explained that $3 billion would only cost the United States about $10 per person, the cost of a movie ticket and a bag of popcorn. Dr. Peter Piot of UN-

AIDS believes that this additional $3 billion would go a long way towards coping with the epidemic in sub-Saharan Africa—with half going to basic care for those already infected, the other half to prevention efforts.

Donors cannot, however, dictate how the battle against AIDS will be fought. A recent report issued by the Africa-America Institute, which champions a greater U.S. commitment to the fight against AIDS in Africa, concludes that donors need to support national priorities set by Africans themselves. Local circumstances vary greatly from country to country, the AAI argues, so international donors need to learn more about Africa and adapt their programs to the needs of each country. "If the U.S. and other donors want to make a difference in the fight against HIV/AIDS in Africa," AAI President Mora McLean says, "they need to listen to Africans and involve them as full partners in the global battle against the epidemic."

Akin Jimoh is a Nigerian science and health writer and a Knight Science Journalism Fellow at the Massachusetts Institute of Technology (MIT) in Cambridge, Massachusetts. He holds two masters degrees, in medical physiology and public health, and has been involved in HIV/AIDS and development work for over 10 years. He is also the program director of Development Communications, a media service nongovernmental organization (NGO) based in Lagos, Nigeria.

Article 24

OUT OF THE ASHES

An interview with Ochoro E. Otunnu, executive director of the New York-based Africa AIDS Initiative.

SUNDAY DARE AND AKIN JIMOH
May/June 2001

Ochoro E. Otunnu is originally from Gulu, Uganda. In 1999, he co-founded the Africa AIDS Initiative (AAI) together with Rory E. Kennedy and Dr. Sorosh Roshan. AAI is a nonprofit organization dedicated to fighting the HIV/AIDS epidemic in Africa by providing technical and financial support to African grassroots and nongovernmental organizations engaged in HIV/AIDS prevention and care. Since 1993, Otunnu has lived in New York City.

The international community, Otunnu says, is not doing enough to fight the HIV/AIDS epidemic that is destroying Africa. Alternative methods, including greater involvement of civil and nongovernmental organizations, greater and cheaper availability of generic drugs, and a more active international community, he argues, are necessary to combat the epidemic. Otunnu radiates hope and confidence that, with sincere and concerted action and inspired leadership from Africa and the international community, Africa will not only survive the crisis, but may emerge from it stronger and more resilient.

Sunday Dare and Akin Jimoh interviewed Otunnu for Dollars & Sense at Harvard University's Kennedy School of Government in November 2000. A Nigerian journalist, Sunday Dare is online editor of The News and Tempo, two leading Lagos-based weeklies. He is currently a Nieman Fellow at Harvard University and a Rockefeller Fellow at D&S. Akin Jimoh is a Nigerian science and health writer and a Knight Science Journalism Fellow at the Massachusetts Institute of Technology in Cambridge, Mass.

Dollars & Sense: What is the central thrust of the Africa AIDS Initiative?

Ochoro E. Otunnu: Our focus, first of all, is on preventing the mother-to-child transmission of HIV by making sure that every expectant mother gets treatment. Second, we're trying to make sure that millions of Africans 18 years or under never get infected. We've got to mount very aggressive prevention campaigns that will make a difference within five years. Finally, every orphan in Africa should get shelter, good health care, and good education. In Africa, our job is to help the community-based organizations that are committed to doing HIV/AIDS work but are not effective because they lack the money, infrastructure, and manpower. Here in the United States we want to do two things. First, we want to mobilize communities to build pressure campaigns like we did during the apartheid era in South Africa. We want to pressure the pharmaceutical companies to cut the cost of drugs to Africa, and to make it possible for African companies to produce generic drugs. We want to bring the cost of AIDS medications down, so no African will be unable to get treatment for lack of money. Second, we want to bring Africa to the center of the foreign-policy debate in this country.

D&S: Why has the AIDS crisis assumed such frightening proportions in Africa?

Otunnu: The first known AIDS cases were in Uganda in 1982. At that time, the overall infection rate for Africa was less than 0.002%. Now there are more than 24 million Africans infected. They represent over 70% of the world's HIV-positive population. Out of 12 million AIDS orphans worldwide, over 90% live in Africa.

In 1988, according to the first global report on HIV/AIDS by the World Health Organization (WHO), there were 68,338 infected people in the United States, 11,445 in Europe, 10,992 in Africa, and 214 in Asia. So the figures have shifted entirely. One of the reasons this happened is that the sexual revolution that happened in the United States in the 1960s has not happened in Africa. The sexual revolution brought greater openness about sex, family planning, and the use of condoms. This meant that when the AIDS epidemic started in the United States, the people were better prepared to respond to it, to do effective prevention campaigns about it. Africa did not have this advantage.

A second factor has been the International Monetary Fund/World Bank policy of structural re-adjustment programs (SAPs). These programs insisted that African governments cut down their budgets, and one of the ways was to reduce social expenditures, health care, and education. So when the AIDS epidemic started, most health-care infrastructure in Africa had been systematically weakened over a number of years.

Finally, in Africa nothing happens until the state OKs it. Most African states, however, have collapsed—Somalia is at war, Nigeria is going through a very turbulent period of transition, other countries face social upheavals. Then you add in bureaucracy, corruption, and most importantly patronage. So the only actor within the country that could have responded to the crisis was unable to respond. It was not prepared. It lacked the leadership to respond quickly and effectively.

African governments did not want to drive out investment and tourism, and they did not want to play into the stereotypes about African sexuality and disease in Africa. These things are part of the colonial legacy, or the colonial myths about Africa. So some of the African leaders with the best intentions did not come out immediately and talk about AIDS because of that. That allowed a period for the disease to spread, because you could not do effective prevention in the media.

D&S: What problems specifically related to Africa do you think are most fundamental in the AIDS crisis?

Otunnu: First is the question of good governance, which basically means transparency and accountability in government. A government that is responsible to its people, so that if you don't provide health care you are kicked out of office. In most African countries, governments don't have to deal with political pressure. In fact, most governments in Africa respond more to pressure from the donor communities than from the pressure from their own people within Africa.

Second is the need to decentralize the state in Africa as the prime deliverer of social goods. And that really is where the international community has to change. International donors keep repeating the same mistakes they made with development in Africa in the last half-century: over-reliance on governments and failing to go directly to the civil and private sector in Africa. You need a combination of humanitarian work—somebody doing it because it is the right thing to do—and the private sector.

D&S: Would you also speak to allegations of Western complicity or ambivalence?

Otunnu: In the West, Africa has been consistently marginalized. Africa doesn't figure among the central foreign policy issues for the United States or Europe. A good example is the Clinton administration, which has professed to be deeply concerned about Africa, but never gave more than $150 million each year for HIV/AIDS prevention in Africa. Only this year has the administration said they would double that amount. Look at what America spends on Israel, over $10 billion a year; on Egypt, about $6 billion annually, I believe—because these countries are part of the Middle Eastern equation. They are at the heart of American foreign policy. And a whole continent of over 600 million people gets less than $150 million a year! Colombia gets over $1 billion to fight drugs!

D&S: Some people argue that Africa needs humanitarian assistance, but when you look at the relationship of the west to Eastern Europe, for example, it's more of a business relationship. Do you think this has an effect on the West committing funds to Africa?

Otunnu: Yes, it has an effect, particularly in the private sector. When Westerners look at African governments they see upheavals and in some instances corruption, and they wonder why they should get involved. Or they look at government budgets and find that not enough is being spent on health compared to the military—so why should they invest money in a sector that is not a priority to an African government? So, what African governments do has a profound impact in terms of private sector behavior and investment.

D&S: What has been your experience as executive director of the Africa AIDS Initiative in terms of campaigns, mobilization, and education?

Otunnu: The experience has been humbling for me. When you find someone who is HIV-positive and see the dignity and courage with which he is living his life, you are humbled by it. It has been inspiring to see the tenacity and resilience of Africans to overcome this enormous problem, in addition to all our other problems. Whatever happens to Africa, whether it is slavery, colonialism, or HIV/AIDS, you can rest assured that Africa will prevail.

I hope for a global mobilization of Africans. There is a huge untapped human capital in Africa and in the diaspora. If we mobilize ourselves in Africa and outside, we can redefine the AIDS debate and change the face of the AIDS epidemic. I think a solution to the AIDS crisis is not going to come from the West; it is going to come from Africa. We need to make a simple declaration. For those of us who were not there during slavery, we look back and wonder how our ancestors could have been conquered by the Europeans for so long. We look at colonialism and we ask how it was possible for Europe to conquer the whole continent. In our own time, AIDS is the biggest challenge, perhaps the biggest challenge ever in our history. Can we be equal to the challenge? We must not allow for a vacuum of leadership at the continental level, at the national level, or at the community level. We can develop leadership like we had in Kwame Nkrumah, Sekou Toure, Jomo Kenyatta and others like them. They went through the crucible of the independence struggle. I hope that a new generation of Africans, confronting the AIDS crisis, will come out with a new level of leadership.

Article 25

SUSTAINABLE SANITATION
A Global Health Challenge

LAURA ORLANDO
May/June 2001

In late October 1995, in the small town of Greenland, New Hampshire, Wheelabrator Water Technologies, Inc. dumped 650 tons of sewage sludge on Rosamond Hughes' field. The sludge contained not only the dregs left over from sewage treatment but also 700 pounds of a nitrogen-based polymer (used to remove water from sludge) and 24,000 pounds of lime. After sitting for several days, the sludge was chain-dragged across the field's surface with a tractor, and then spread repeatedly for the next three weeks. As it dried, it was blown by steady winds toward the home of 26-year-old Shayne Conner, just 300 feet away.

Almost immediately, Conner, his family, and their neighbors began to get sick. Overcome by the stench, they started vomiting. They felt burning sensations in their eyes, throats, and lungs. They experienced nosebleeds, headaches, congestion, fever, and nausea, and they had difficulty breathing. And then, on a quiet day in November—less than one month after the sludge was dumped on the Hughes' property—Shayne Conner died.

When sanitation is practiced successfully, it can promote health and prevent disease. But its effectiveness depends on many factors—education, behavioral changes, access to clean water, solid and industrial waste management, and the safe disposition of human excreta. What happened to Shayne Conner is just one tragic example of how, in rich as well as poor countries, improper sanitation can cause environmental degradation, illness, and death.

Rich Nation, Poor Sanitation

In rich countries, sewers and sewage treatment systems are considered signs of progress, but they are the reason we have toxic sludge. First comes the sewage, a mixture of undifferentiated industrial and household wastes. Then there's the treatment process, which attempts to clean the wastewater that the sewage contains. What's left over—after the dead cats and cardboard are screened out and hauled away to the dump—is a concoction of whatever was flushed down the drain: motor oil, dioxin, asbestos, polychlorinated biphenyls (PCBs), heavy metals, bacteria, viruses, industrial solvents, any combination of the 70,000 chemicals used in U.S. industries, and so on. And the better the water at the end of the treatment cycle, the nastier the sludge will be.

At one time, sludge's pungent smell was considered offensive only on aesthetic grounds. But new research in the Journal of Agromedicine confirms that sludge's olfactory assault can have serious physical health consequences as well. So, while it might seem safe and convenient to have our waste whisked out of sight, we're paying the piper at the end of the pipe.

In spite of sludge's poisonous properties, the federal government keeps calling it a fertilizer and putting it on land. The Environmental Protection Agency (EPA) is in charge of regulating the disposal of sewage sludge. Since 1992, when Congress banned the practice of dumping sludge in the ocean, the EPA has geared its regulations and public relations efforts toward one goal: To dump sludge wherever possible, primarily on U.S. farmland. That's the cheapest way to dispose of sludge and launder the toxic waste that goes into sewers. The EPA now goes to great lengths to convince people that sludge makes good fertilizer. For instance, the agency refers to sludge as "biosolids"—the winning entry in a 1990 contest sponsored by the sewage industry to make its main product more marketable.

Despite the preponderance of pro-sludge propaganda, however, not everyone is fooled. When Shayne Conner's mother, Joanne Marshall, filed a wrongful death suit against Wheelabrator, Dr. David Lewis—an EPA microbiologist and whistleblower—testified in the case. According to Lewis, the symptoms reported by Greenland, New Hampshire, residents were "consistent with a growing number of cases where people have been exposed to airborne contaminants from land-applied sewage sludge." It was well-established in the scientific and medical literature, Lewis noted, that "inhaling of irritant gases and pathogen-contaminated, limed sludge dust" could "lead to infections of respiratory and gastrointestinal systems and serious, life-threatening complications."

Why, then, is the United States so invested in the sewers and sewage treatment plants that produce toxic sludge? Since passage of the Clean Water Act in 1972, many communities have had no choice but to put in sewers and build expensive sewage treatment plants. The resulting multi-billion dollar sewering effort created a powerful wastewater industry. The EPA, while ostensibly charged with protecting the environment, caters to that industry and other corporate interests.

What we do with sludge now is a public health and environmental disaster. Instead, sludge should be treated as hazardous waste. We need to promote public policies that aim to reduce its production, by not extending existing sewers or building new ones. In addition, source separation should be the mantra of the EPA (and you and me): Keeping waste products separate at the point of production will greatly facilitate safe recycling and reuse.

Sanitation Crisis in the Global South

In the wealthiest country in the world, people are dying from the industrial end product of state-of-the-art sewage treatment systems. In the Global South, where 65% of the population have no sanitation facilities at all, people are dying from exposure to excreta that carry disease.

The state of global sanitation, according to Akhtar Hameed Khan, is "unconscionable." Khan is the director of the Orangi Pilot Project, a low-cost sanitation project that has reached thousands of people in Karachi, Pakistan. "On the brink of the 21st century," he wrote in Progress of Nations, a 1997 UNICEF study, "half the world's people are enduring a medieval level of sanitation. Almost 3 billion individuals do not have access to a decent toilet, and many of them are forced to defecate on the bare ground or queue up to pay for the use of a filthy latrine."

The "medieval level of sanitation," Khan points out, results in a "medieval level of disease." The improper management of human excreta wreaks havoc on people's health in both rich and poor countries. But its consequences are most brutal for poor people in developing nations, where it results in the deaths of 2.2 million children each year. In densely settled areas where there is no containment of human waste, disease-causing organisms—primarily found in feces—easily move from one person to the next. (Water is the ideal but by no means the only conduit.) These organisms cause many illnesses, including diarrhoeal diseases, which are responsible for killing the majority of children who die before reaching the age of five. In addition to promulgating disease and degrading water and soil quality, the lack of ecological excreta management is a dignity issue in people's everyday lives.

When it comes to investing in environment sanitation, however, bringing health and dignity to poor people is not high on the list. The lion's share of such investment goes to sewerage in urban areas, subsidizing services for industrial development, the middle class, and the rich. According to the United Nations, in 2000, only 34% of rural residents in developing countries had access to sanitation, compared with 80% of urban residents. During the UN-declared International Water and Sanitation Decade (1980-1990), funding for sanitation skyrocketed. But according to Frank Hartvelt, deputy director of the Science and Technology Private Sector Division of the UN Development Programme, 80% of all investment went to "well-off urban areas, for expensive installations." As in wealthy countries, it is those with the most economic clout who decide what kinds of public services will be provided, and who will benefit from the expenditure of public funds.

These same priorities determine what types of solutions the world's sanitation "experts" devise. In 1998, the UN set up the World Water Commission to examine water issues. In its Vision Report, published last year, the Commission identified what it called "a vital need for high tech innovation." As an example of this, the Report suggested "the use of computer chips to control the digestion process in smart-composting toilets." Good for Intel—bad for the three billion people without any toilet. The digestion process in composting toilets needs carbon—chopped leaves, wood chips—not silicon. But then again, they wouldn't be able to add and subtract.

People in the Global South live in a world rich enough to afford a universal level of sanitation that would help to protect their health. But regardless of how much money is available, we will trade one set of problems for another unless we radically rethink how that money is spent.

A Model for Sustainable Sanitation

The truth is, neither sewers nor computer chips in composting toilets are functionally or environmentally sustainable. Instead, what is needed are sanitation systems that keep toxic and human wastes separate, prevent pollution, and return the nutrients in urine and feces to the soil as fertilizers. Small projects have demonstrated systems that accomplish these goals while also being culturally appropriate, locally responsible, affordable, functional, and even beautiful.

One example can be found on the Caribbean coast of Mexico, a fragile ecosystem that is home to 554,000 people and four million tourists. Since 1993, the ReSource Institute for Low Entropy Systems (RILES), a nonprofit concerned with sanitation, has built about 300 composting toilets in the Yucatan Peninsula. Most are paid for by their owners: maids, gardeners, masons, carpenters, schoolteachers, doctors, editors, tourism operators, hotels, municipalities, and retired Americans, to name a few. All of them are functioning well. Word has spread that they have no smell, do not fill up, can be in the house or outside, and can be hooked to a water toilet or not; that there is somebody around who knows how to maintain them; and that there are people who will gladly take away and use the fertilizer that these systems produce. The fact that these composting toilets are also beautiful is no small part of their success. The first few were built in houses with dirt floors, but soon people with beachfront homes wanted them. Because of their aesthetic appeal, the toilets have won acceptance across class boundaries. In an effort to build a local infrastructure to keep up with demand and maintain quality control, RILES has helped establish three Mexican corporations: a company to prefabricate the composting toilets; a workers' cooperative to maintain them and build the bathrooms that go on top; and a nonprofit organization to carry out education and policy-related work. (The author is director of RILES.)

Another project is in Cuernavaca, in central Mexico, where an architect named César Añorvé has been promoting two chamber (double-vault) dry toilets. (One chamber is used until full, then left to dehydrate while the other is used.) Añorvé has added an entrepreneurial element to his efforts by designing and selling attractive toilet fixtures. He collaborates with a nonprofit organization, Espacio de Salud, and together they have made the double-vault toilet widely available, with the construction supervision and maintenance necessary to build them correctly and keep them functioning properly.

Why not just hand out blueprints and leave it at that? It doesn't work. It has been demonstrated over and over again that there is an infinite number of ways to build a composting toilet so that it does not function well. Training and supervision take care of this. Regular maintenance keeps the toilets working. Homeowners need support for these things. Add to this the fact that there is a social change element to the project, and you can see why a blueprint won't do the trick.

Though do-it-yourself construction can be an effective way to get some on-site systems built for low-income households, many other components are needed to bring these efforts to scale. Providing sustainable sanitation technologies for billions of people will require replacing the existing engineering and financial infrastructure that currently supports sewerage with one that supports ecological innovations in waste treatment. That, in turn, will require massive government and organizational—for-profit sometimes, nonprofit other times, a combination of both most of the time—intervention. And whatever the technology, people will have to want it.

What is needed is a new approach consisting of:

- Principles that put source separation first in the decision-making hierarchy;
- People who approach sanitation from both a health and ecological perspective;
- Financing—both private and public—to develop production and marketing

capabilities;
- Easy access by those who want sustainable sanitation technologies to those who can deliver, install, and maintain them;
- Financial packages to help people pay for toilets; and
- Government policies that punish polluters, reward ecological innovators, and promote and help pay for universal sustainable sanitation coverage.

The fact that half of the people in the world do not have a toilet reflects government priorities that are politically and morally bankrupt. The fact that the other half has little or no access to sustainable sanitation reflects misconceptions about conventional sanitation systems and what they can and cannot do. Under the current system, everyone suffers. But it doesn't have to be that way.

Laura Orlando is a member of the Dollars & Sense *collective and the director of the Re-Source Institute for Low Entropy Systems (www.riles.org), a non-profit concerned with public health and the environment. Part of her work for the past 13 years has been to develop composting toilet projects.*

Article 26

PUTTING NAMES ON THE NUMBERS
Testimonies of the Uninsured

LISA CLIMAN AND ADRIA SCHARF
May/June 2001

The United States is the only modern industrialized country without a sound health insurance program. In 1999, one in six non-elderly U.S. residents – more than 42.5 million people – went without health coverage for the entire year. During the economic boom of the 1990s, the number of uninsured actually grew, both in terms of raw numbers and in terms of their proportion of the total population.

Don't expect the situation to improve any time soon. Even with a vast budget surplus at their disposal, neither Republicans nor Democrats plan to increase public spending for social needs. Instead, they want to spend the surplus on tax cuts and paying down the national debt. Either way, the outlook remains bleak for those living without health coverage, and for recipients of Medicaid and Medicare as well.

Below are the highlights from the Kaiser Commission on Medicaid and the Uninsured's new report, In Their Own Words: The Uninsured Talk About Living Without Health Insurance. The report profiles eight families who cannot afford the coverage they need. As a result, they postpone medical care, live in pain, worry, and take n crushing debt when they inevitably do seek medical attention. The full report can be downloaded at www.kff.org/kcmu. —Lisa Climan and Adria Scharf

The Smith Family, Paterson, NJ

Each time a fever struck one of her daughters during the two anxious years when they didn't have health insurance, Yolanda Smith would ask herself a series of questions: How high was the temperature? What could she do to bring it down? Was it serious enough to require a doctor's attention?

If the fever persisted, Yolanda might wait it out one more day. If it still hadn't come down, she would reluctantly borrow $40 from her mother to pay the fee that the doctor's office required up front. If her mother didn't have the money, Yolanda would play her last card and take her daughter to the emergency room, knowing that the bill for that visit, though huge, would drift in later.

Like the majority of uninsured Americans, Yolanda, 29, works full-time, in her case as a customer service representative for a cigar-distribution company. Part of the appeal of Yolanda's new job was that it offered health insurance. But Yolanda suffered a sticker shock when she found out what her share of the cost would be. To cover herself alone, she had to pay $85 every two weeks. Coverage that would include her daughters would have cost $150 every two weeks, an amount she simply could not figure out a way to pay.

Yolanda earns $12.50 an hour, or about $26,000 a year. That puts her squarely in the hardscrabble territory of low income America, defined as those who earn less than 200% of the federal poverty level, or $28,300 for a family of three in 2000. It is these workers and their families, living just a few handholds above poverty, that run the second highest risk, after the poor, of being uninsured.

The Nelson Family, Louisville, Tenn.

Nobody needs to tell Patricia Nelson how important health insurance is. When her husband William was just 35 years old, he developed Lou Gehrig's disease. The disability-linked insurance provided by Medicare meant that in the final months of his illness, Patricia could care for him in their own home, with doctors, nurses, and therapists stopping by as needed, at little cost to the family.

Despite Patricia's understanding of the significance of insurance, she and her

---

Who Are the Uninsured?

Most are people who work, or their dependents. Over two-thirds (71%) come from families with at least one full-time worker. Only 18% come from families where no one is employed.

Many are not poor. Over a third (35%) come from families with incomes above 200% of the poverty line. Just under a third (29%) come from near-poor families, with incomes between 100 and 200% of the poverty line. Thirty-six percent come from families with incomes below the poverty line ($13,290 for a family of three in 1999).

Three quarters (75%) are adults. Because of government insurance programs that target children, adults are at greater risk of being uninsured than children.

Half of the uninsured are white, but minorities, particularly Hispanics, are at much greater risk of being uninsured than whites.

Source: The Kaiser Commission on Medicaid and the Uninsured, Health Insurance Coverage in America: 1999 Data Update.

son Sam have been going without it since June 2000, one month after she left a job with health benefits to help a sister and brother-in-law strengthen their family business.

Like many Americans, Patricia has found over the years that her family's access to health insurance has depended largely on the decisions of employers. For 10 years, from 1983 through 1993, Patricia worked in a restaurant, making just above minimum wage. "Sometimes there was insurance, sometimes there wasn't, depending on who the owners were," she says.

The most costly uninsured medical expense came when Sam was five years old and had a bad asthma attack. At Children's Hospital, the billing office checked on whether Sam was eligible for Medicaid. Patricia remembers the family missing the eligibility cutoff by $4. "We were in there for two days, and I ended up with a $6,000 hospital bill that I'm still paying $25 a month on," Patricia says. Her balance, after seven years of paying, is $1,790.

She prays that she and Sam stay healthy and injury-free. "The thing is, you can't get private insurance for a price you can afford," she says.

Note: After the Kaiser report was issued, Patricia Nelson lost her job when her sister's business closed down. She has since developed a serious kidney infection, and Sam now has Bell's Palsy. Faced with over $12,000 in medical bills, she has filed for bankruptcy.

The Pafford Family, Elon, Va.

Through the years, Tom, now 46, has worked hard to provide for his family. He's worked at lots of different jobs – as an assistant minister, a sheet metal fabricator, a Hawaiian Punch can assembler, a machine mechanic, a painter, and a construction supervisor. Not all of those jobs provided him with health insurance, though. In fact, he and his family often weren't covered. They paid for health care as they needed it and put off what they could.

The Paffords don't believe they're owed anything – not by the government, not by employers. But Tom would like to see companies take more responsibility for their employees. He remembers what it was like growing up in New Jersey, where his father, a union electrical worker, always had good employer-provided health insurance for his whole family. Tom also remembers his own experiences with employers that provided good coverage. "We were well taken care of," he recalls. But as time went on, those kinds of jobs have become harder to find.

"It may be wrong on my part," he says, "but I think an employer as large as mine—a medical corporation—could do something for its employees, like my father had or like I once had."

Lisa Climan is an undergraduate at Boston University and a D&S *intern. Adria Scharf is a member of the* D&S *collective.*

Article 27

MAKING PATIENTS PAY
U.S. Health System Puts Profits First

ELLEN FRANK
May/June 2001

When Cynthia Herdrich visited her primary-care physician complaining of abdominal pain, the doctor scheduled an ultrasound for eight days later and sent her home. Shortly thereafter, Herdrich's appendix ruptured, causing a life-threatening infection and requiring emergency surgery. Only during the subsequent malpractice suit did Herdrich discover that her insurer, Carle Care HMO of Urbana, Illinois, instructed its doctors to delay, as a matter of course, diagnostic tests for seven days in the hope that either the symptoms or the patient would go away. Physicians who saved the plan money received year-end bonuses.

Herdrich's case, which became national news when the Supreme Court ruled that she could not sue the health maintenance organization (HMO), exemplified everything Americans have come to hate and fear about the medical system: the greedy insurers concerned more with saving money than saving lives; the deceitful providers secretly committed to withholding care to boost their own incomes; the maddening laws allowing insurance companies to dictate medical decisions, but shielding them from legal liability when things go wrong. Above all, though, Herdrich's case—in which the HMO allowed a serious but uncomplicated condition to progress to a dangerous situation requiring lengthy hospitalization and extensive surgery—highlights the sheer wastefulness of managed care.

The Bad Old Days of Fee-For-Service Medicine

It wasn't supposed to be like this. When large employers began contracting with managed-care firms (insurance plans that "manage" patient treatment, usually by requiring that procedures be ordered only through a primary-care doctor and pre-approved by the insurer) in the late 1980s, boosters argued that the HMOs would restrain costs and wring waste out of the medical system by emphasizing preventive care and proven remedies.

Few denied that the system needed fixing. By the end of the 1980s, the U.S. health-care system was the world's most costly, even though millions of Americans went without medical care altogether. Most people obtained medical insurance privately through their employer. Medicare and Medicaid, federal programs enacted in 1965, covered the elderly and the very poor. Until recently, private insurance plans, as well as the federal health programs, were organized as fee-for-service plans. Consumers chose a doctor, the doctor prescribed treatments and set a fee, and the insurer paid the bills.

Under the fee-for-service system, physicians were quick to recognize that their incomes rose directly with the number of services they performed. American doctors performed invasive tests and procedures at rates far exceeding international norms. Caesarean sections, rare in Europe, accounted by 1990 for nearly a quarter of all births in the United States. American gastroenterologists treated ulcers with invasive tests, ineffectual antacids, and frequent office visits long after doctors abroad had shown that most ulcers were easily treatable with antibiotics. U.S. surgeons performed hysterectomies and tonsillectomies at rates far above their international counterparts. In the 1980s, John Wennberg, author of the annual Dartmouth Atlas of Health Care, found that in some regions, two-thirds of all children had had their tonsils removed.

"Kickbacks" for diagnostic tests and referrals encouraged frequent and extensive testing. Physicians often sent patients for X-rays and other tests at facilities they themselves owned. In 1989, Congress directed Medicare to withhold payment for tests using equipment owned by the referring doctor, but such self-referrals continued to plague the industry, driving up costs and feeding a widespread disgust with the medical profession.

From 1960 to 1990, increases in physicians' incomes outpaced inflation virtually every year and overall health-care expenditures rose two to three times faster than the nation's income. The average medical doctor in the United States earns $200,000—seven times the average annual wage. Doctors' groups like the American Medical Association (AMA) opposed virtually every effort to reform the system. In a 1993 survey commissioned by the AMA, 44% of those polled agreed that "doctors think they are better than other people," 69% said doctors were too interested in money, and 67% believed doctors' fees were too high. Seventy percent said they were beginning to "lose faith in doctors."

The Managed Care Revolution

By the close of the 1980s, medical-insurance premiums were rising by 15% per year. Critics noted that the United States spent more money per person on health care than any other country, yet in many cases fared worse on measures of health, like life expectancy and infant mortality rates. Over 40 million U.S. residents, most of them working people, have no medical coverage at all because their employers do not provide coverage and they cannot afford to pay the skyrocketing premiums. Clinton's 1992 election campaign promised health-care reform. With the defeat of the Clinton health plan, however, "market forces" swept through the industry, hawking managed care to employers who were incensed with the soaring cost of medical insurance.

Employers balked at a system under which doctors raised their fees, insurers raised their premiums, and businesses paid the freight. Many firms cut employee health coverage altogether or passed costs on to their employees, but this strategy had limitations. Federal legislation generally requires that firms provide fringe benefits like health insurance to all employees—executives and factory operatives alike—or to none. Furthermore, employment-based medical coverage tied workers to their jobs. Despite spiraling costs, employer organizations like the National Association of Manufacturers consistently oppose national health programs, even as they object to the cost of private insurance.

As a group, employers tend to place great faith in profit-driven enterprise to solve social problems, so they were particularly receptive to promises by insurers that managed care could trim the fat from the medical system. In 1985, fewer than one in ten U.S. residents was enrolled in a managed-care plan. Today 90% of those with employment-based health insurance have managed-care plans. Also known as HMOs, managed-care firms originated as non-profit pre-paid plans maintaining their own clinics and salaried physicians. Today, most HMOs are operated by for-profit insurance firms like Aetna, whose US Healthcare HMO enrolls 10% of HMO members nationally.

The appeal of managed care to employers is simple. The HMO contracts with a group (or "network") of physicians, diagnostic labs, and hospitals to provide care for all of its members. Providers in the network, guaranteed the business of the HMO members, agree to accept sharply discounted reimbursement rates. HMO members are generally not allowed to visit providers outside the network. In addition, members must obtain their primary-care doctor's consent before using any other provider—even emergency rooms. The HMO saves money both by negotiating discounted fees and by restricting the services that members use.

Discounting Fees

Doctors, labs, and hospitals need insured patients, but insurers also need providers. To strengthen their respective bargaining positions, both providers and insurers are merging, combining, and reorganizing at a furious pace. Insurers were first to recognize the advantages of concentration. The early 1990s saw a wave of mergers and acquisitions among health insurers that left large regions of the country with only two or three competing health plans. Their superior bargaining power allowed insurers to negotiate sharp reductions in fees, which were passed on to employers in the form of lower premiums. In 1994, the average health-insurance premium fell for the first time in years; premiums increased at or below the inflation rate for the rest of the 1990s.

Hospitals, facing lower reimbursement rates, cut staff and beds for traditional inpatient care while expanding facilities for expensive services like outpatient surgery. Still, hospitals throughout the country suffered operating losses. Large urban hospitals in low-income areas were especially hard-hit, because federal law requires hospitals to treat anyone who shows up at the emergency room. For-profit hospital chains—promising deep pockets, access to capital markets, and the market clout to bargain with insurers—moved in quickly, buying up scores of non-profit community hospitals.

Founded in 1988, HCA Healthgroup, the nation's largest for-profit chain, now owns around 300 hospitals. Tenet Healthcare, owner of 110 hospitals in 17 states, has recently gone on an acquisition spree, targeting hospitals, says the *Wall Street Journal*, "in financial trouble, a plight that characterizes more than one-third of the nation's 5000 hospitals."

In many cases, the sale of non-profit hospitals enriches the physicians and hospital board members who broker the deals. David Himmelstein, of the Ad Hoc Committee to Defend Health Care, says "it's not clear to what extent for-profit hospital conversions are driven by economic factors like access to capital markets and to what extent the managers of non-profits are virtually bribed to convert and get a huge payoff."

Where hospitals have remained non-profit, they have merged and combined with physician groups and laboratories to form powerful negotiating blocs. Partners Healthcare of Massachusetts, for example, includes hospitals, diagnostic labs, and physician groups that together treat around one-quarter of Boston-area patients. Last fall, Partners flexed its considerable muscle by announcing that its providers would no longer treat members of Tufts HMO—which itself enrolls nearly 20% of the state's insured—unless Tufts substantially raised reimbursement rates. The HMO swiftly capitulated. Himmelstein points out that, under pressure from insurers, non-profit hospitals "over the long-term have to duplicate what the for-profits do."

The solo physician practice and free-standing community hospital are rapidly vanishing, replaced by behemoths like Partners. Managed care has also spawned a new breed of for-profit firms like PhyCor, Inc., a national chain of physician groups that, in return for a management fee of 10-15%, negotiates fees and handles insurance paperwork for the doctors.

Consolidation and integration riddle the medical industry with conflicts of interest. HCA is under federal investigation for investing in physician practices in exchange for patient referrals, a violation of Medicare anti-kickback rules. Pharmaceutical giant AstraZeneca, a manufacturer of chemotherapy drugs, owns Salick Health Care, which runs cancer treatment clinics throughout the country.

Analysts estimate that managed-care insurers spend 80-85% of premiums reimbursing providers. The remaining 15-20% covers the insurers' administrative and marketing costs and, of course, their profits. When we add the profits of drug companies, hospitals, labs, and physician groups, the costs of marketing lucrative out-of-pocket services, and the costs of sending bills and processing referral forms—it is likely that as much as one-third of "health-care" spending is skimmed off as profit or as sheer waste. This may explain why Americans spend nearly twice as much per capita on health care as the Japanese yet live, on average, four years less.

Restricting Care

In the ideal of managed care, advanced by health-care economists like Alain Enthoven and Paul Ellwood, cost-conscious payers were supposed to work with primary care doctors to design cost-effective treatment plans, avoiding the over-treatment endemic to fee-for-service medicine. Managed-care companies would have the authority and the incentive to practice preventive medicine, encouraging members to join health clubs, quit smoking, and get regular check-ups. Primary-care doctors, long denigrated by a profession that exalted specialists, would be newly empowered to resist unnecessary treatments.

But pressure to cut expenditures instead thrust primary-care physicians, with little preparation, into a financial and bureaucratic morass. Having agreed to lower payments and facing mounting administrative costs, physicians simply cut the one variable still in their control—time spent with patients. The average length of an office visit, never a leisurely affair, is now just around 10 minutes. Time spent overseeing complex cases, not to mention checking that people received routine care or tests, never materialized. Studies indicate that primary and preventive care have deteriorated under managed care. Commenting in his most recent survey of the U.S. health system, John Wennberg complained that "there are no systems in place for doctors to take care of patient populations ... primary care is chaotically organized."

A recent study for the health policy journal *Milbank Quarterly* concluded that "whether the care is preventive, acute or chronic, [the U.S. health-care system] frequently does not meet professional standards."

Even well-organized preventive care cannot overcome the reality that the medical industry basically exists to care for the sick, not the healthy. Two-thirds of all medical expenses are incurred by 10% of the population. In every age group, 1% of the population accounts for about 30% of expenditures. Cutting expenditures inevitably entails reducing what the industry euphemistically calls "medical losses"—payments to treat the sick. Insurers have thus introduced rules intended to discourage treatment. Some are explicit, limiting hospitalization after an uncomplicated birth to 24 hours, or delaying diagnostic tests except in medical emergencies. More often, though, insurers impede care by requiring doctors to get authorization for all tests and procedures or by threatening to drop doctors whose costs they deem excessive.

Most controversial are reimbursement agreements that place the economic interests of physicians in direct conflict with their responsibility to patients. Many insurers pay doctors a fixed annual fee supplemented by a year-end bonus if the physician "spends" less than the average on patient care. Others employ "capitation" agreements, under which primary-care physicians receive a fixed fee for each covered member. Because the annual payment represents a budget that must cover all the expenses associated with those plan members, including office visits, diagnostic tests, and treatment by specialists, capitation shifts the financial risk of treating very sick patients from the insurer to the physician. One or two complex cases, if fully treated, can substantially cut into a practice's income.

Many insurers bar participating physicians from disclosing the terms of their contracts, either privately to patients or in public venues. In 1995, David Himmelstein, well-known critic of for-profit HMOs, was famously dropped from US Healthcare after criticizing the HMO on the Phil Donahue Show. Subsequently, Massachusetts and a few other states passed legislation prohibiting such "gag clauses" in HMO contracts, but the practice remains legal in most states.

Profit-Driven Medicine

Last fall, newspapers reported that urban emergency rooms across the country were turning ambulances away at record rates, the fallout from several years of cutbacks in hospital staff and facilities. Non-profit hospitals, having discounted rates to secure the business of managed-care firms, are under intense pressure to cut costs and trim staff, just like the for-profit chains. In a move echoed by strapped non-profits across the country, Beth Israel Deaconess Hospital of Boston, a Harvard Medical School teaching hospital, announced plans to partner with a pharmaceutical company that would exploit discoveries by the hospital research staff. While conceding the potential for conflicts of interest, hospital officials insisted that they had to find some source of revenue to stanch annual losses in the hundreds of millions of dollars.

Defenders of for-profit medicine contend that the marketplace is working well. Managed care, they point out, did succeed in restraining medical inflation during much of the 1990s. And while critics maintain that cost reductions have come at the expense of patient care, industry defenders counter that offices established recently in several states to investigate consumer complaints about managed care are languishing for lack of business. Spokespeople for managed care point to surveys in which 80% of those polled express satisfaction with their health-care plan. They insist that the industry is getting a bum rap—that criticisms are based more on perception than reality.

But in a sensitive field like medicine, perception and reality cannot be so neatly separated. A person who is sick or injured has neither the knowledge nor the emotional distance to function as a rational consumer. Patients must rely absolutely on the disinterest and integrity of those who make decisions about their care. When the quest for profit pervades medical care, whether driven by physician-entrepreneurs or by managed-care shareholders, it so poisons public trust that even reasonable treatment restrictions (like limiting use of experimental bone-marrow transplants) invite cynicism and lawsuits.

An ideal health-care system would certainly require rationing of care. America probably devotes too many resources on heroic end-of-life interventions and not enough on long-term and rehabilitative care, too much on designer drugs and too little on childhood vaccinations, too much on the rich and too little on the uninsured. How to allocate scarce medical resources is a topic worthy of debate, but that debate needs to take place in public, not in corporate boardrooms and secret negotiations between insurers and providers.

Ellen Frank teaches at Emmanuel College in Boston and is a member of the Dollars & Sense *collective.*

Article 28

SPENDING #1, PERFORMANCE #37
How U.S. Health Care Stacks Up Internationally

PHINEAS BAXANDALL
May/June 2001

Overall, the United States spends about 50% more per capita on health care than any other country. The private sector accounts for about 56% of total health spending in the United States, compared to an average of 25% in other industrialized countries. At the same time, *public* health spending per capita is higher in the United States than in any other wealthy capitalist country except Switzerland, Luxembourg, and Germany. You would think that with our unrivalled levels of spending, Americans would be the healthiest people on earth. But our health-care system is abysmally inefficient when it comes to delivering health.

A path-breaking new report from the World Health Organization (WHO) studies and ranks how 191 countries, from Afghanistan to Zimbabwe, provide health care. Researchers compared each country's achievements to the resources available in that country. Then they ranked this performance against that of other countries. The WHO based its assessments on five categories: over-all population health, health inequalities, health system responsiveness (based on patient satisfaction, waiting periods, etc.), distribution of responsiveness (how well the system serves people of differing economic status), and distribution of costs.

The WHO gives the United States high marks for its world-class doctor training and advanced medical technology. And the United States tops the list in "responsiveness" for virtues like confidentiality, brief waiting periods, and patient decision-making autonomy. But overall, the United States ranks 37th in national performance, behind not only most European nations and Japan, but also Chile, Colombia, Saudi Arabia, and Singapore.

American health-care performance is weighed down by its shabby provision for the 16% of citizens who are not insured. According to the Henry J. Kaiser Family Foundation, uninsured people are more likely to miss recommended medical tests and treatments. Uninsured children are 30% less likely to receive treatment after an injury. And death rates for uninsured women with breast cancer are 40-60% higher than for insured women, after adjusting for age, income, and race.

Even for those with insurance, the U.S. system does worse in many ways than other countries'. While few U.S. doctors make house calls, such visits are common and inexpensive in Italy, France, and Germany. "Patients in countries like France and Germany have more doctors' visits, specialist care and hospital time than their counterparts elsewhere," the *Wall Street Journal* admits. "Permission isn't needed to see a specialist or get a second opinion, and weeklong trips to the spa are not uncommon treatment in Germany." Not so under the United States' "managed care" system.

Profit drives the U.S. system, and what is most profitable for hospitals, insurance companies, or drug companies is not most effective at producing good health. Much of the United States' "health-care spending" goes to company profits, multimillion dollar CEO salaries, and marketing. The health industry focuses on people with the greatest ability to pay rather than the greatest need for care. Private healthcare spending therefore goes disproportionately toward expensive eleventh-hour measures unlikely to extend life for very long and to pricey lifestyle drugs such as Rogaine. Lack of access to basic care, in turn, makes for costly system-wide inefficiencies. When poor women cannot get basic prenatal care, for example, they and their newborns are more likely to suffer complications requiring around-the-clock intensive care. When uninsured people are unable to see a general practitioner, they must often rely on expensive emergency-room care.

How do higher-ranked health-care systems work? There is no single answer.

HEALTH CARE SYSTEMS AT A GLANCE
By Alkin Gorgun

	Canada	France	Germany	Japan	Spain	Sweden	United Kingdom
What is the basic type of health care system?	Single-payer	Multi-payer	Multi-payer	Single-payer	National health service	Single-payer	National health service
What are the key dates?	1944—first provincial health insurance program (Saskatchewan).	1927—system established; 1978—universal coverage.	1883—world's first public health insurance system.	1958—system established.	1978—new constitution declares right to health care; system established.	1962—system established.	1948—system established.
Who administers health-care services?	Provinces; federal oversight	Sickness Insurance Funds (SIFs)	Sickness Insurance Funds (SIFs)	Local governments	National Institute of Health	County councils	National Health Service
Who pays for services?	National insurance system, 72% of total. Funded by general taxation.	SIFs, 75% of total. Funded by payroll taxes (13% of wage; employers pay 70%, employees 30%).	SIFs, 81% of total. Funded by payroll taxes (14% of wage; employers pay 50%, employees 50%).	Insurance premiums paid to local governments, 57%; federal government, 24%; local governments, 7%.	National health service. Funded by payroll taxes (employers pay 75%; employees, 25%).	County taxes, 72% of total.	National health service, 88% of total. Funded by general taxation and insurance premiums.
Who owns the hospitals? How are they run?	Mainly private non-profit.	Private, both non-profit and for-profit.	Mainly public, many private non-profit, some private for-profit.	Mainly private non-profit. Investor-owned hospitals prohibited.	Public hospitals run by national health service, provinces, or municipalities.	Public hospitals, run by country councils.	Mainly self-governing public trusts.

Sources: Information is primarily from Physicians for a National Health Program (www.pnhp.org). Also from the European Observatory on Health Care Systems (www.observatory.dk).

Alkin Gorgun is a Dollars & Sense *intern.*

The systems of countries #1 (France) to #36 (Costa Rica) differ on how the costs are split up, how physicians are paid, who owns the hospitals, what is the role of primary-care doctors, and who pays for pharmaceuticals, among other features. The systems, however, fall into three broad categories. First, there are universal multi-payer systems in countries like Germany and France. While these countries have multiple "sickness insurance funds," their health systems differ greatly from the United States' private-insurance system. The insurance funds in France and Germany are funded by taxes rather than insurance premiums and are tightly regulated by their governments. Then there are single-payer systems such as in Canada and Sweden. In these countries, the government offers a single insurance system that provides coverage to all citizens. Finally, there are countries, such as Great Britain and Spain, which have national health services. Unlike the others, these are not insurance systems at all. Instead, the government owns hospitals and employs health-care providers directly. Even under single-payer or national-health systems, private insurance companies may offer supplemental coverage.

For all their differences, other countries publicly regulate the provision of health care more closely than the United States. Defenders of the U.S. system often decry these alternatives as forms of "rationing" and "bureaucracy." The United States, however, already has plenty of both, courtesy of the private, profit-driven system. Every HMO or managed-care arrangement in the United States rations care—permitting a patient to see a specialist only if referred by a primary-care physician, refusing to cover certain treatments altogether—while the system as a whole rations care according to ability to pay. And even the *Wall Street Journal* admits that the U.S. system "has accumulated a massive bureaucracy that simply doesn't exist in other countries." Perhaps one fourth of so-called "heath care" workers "do nothing but paperwork."

It should not come as any surprise that, for our unmatched levels of spending, the United States gets less than it pays for. What the U.S. system has—inefficiency, red tape, and big profits—is expensive. What it lacks—universal coverage—is priceless.

Phineas Baxandall is a member of the Dollars & Sense *collective.*

RESOURCES: World Health Organization, *World Health Report 2000, Health Systems: Improving performance* (www.who.into/whr/2000/en/report.htm); *The Wall Street Journal*, Special Health and Medicine Supplement, February 21, 2001; Universal Healthcare Action Network (www.uhcan.org); Physicians for a National health Program (www.pnhp.org); The European Observatory on Health Care Systems (www.observatory.dk/frame_index_main.htm).

Article 29
MEDICAL RESIDENTS ORGANIZE
STEPHANIE GREENWOOD
May/June 2001

On March 23, residents at St. Luke's-Roosevelt Hospital in Manhattan voted overwhelmingly to join the Committee of Interns and Residents (CIR), affiliated with the Services Employees International Union (SEIU). The final tally was 283 to 44.

The St. Luke's-Roosevelt victory represents the first successful union drive at a private hospital since the National labor Relations Board (NLRB) ruled, in 1999, that residents are primarily employees. Residents (a term that covers interns, residents, and fellows) are physicians who have finished medical school but are not yet licensed; during residency, they develop expertise in specialized areas, like cardiology or internal medicine. Previously, the NLRB had classified them as students.

The rise of organizing among such "professionals" reflects just how serious the impact of market forces on health care has become. At private hospitals, as at public ones, residents face worsening conditions: They typically put in more than 80 hours a week for salaries amounting to between $6 and $12 an hour, while paying huge loans and often raising families. Residents are responsible for front-line patient care and often pick up the slack as hospitals cut support staff and reduce resources and training time. Dependent on the institution for their licenses, their jobs, and (for many immigrants) their visas, residents are uniquely exploitable.

Under pressure from privatization and other forms of market encroachment, residents are increasingly joining the labor movement. Just five years ago, CIR/SEIU had fewer than 7,000 members, most of them in public hospitals where workers had forced management to recognize the union. Today, the union represents more than 11,000 residents in New York, Massachusetts, California, Florida, New Jersey, and Washington, D.C. Since the 1999 decision, it had launched new organizing campaigns, mostly at private hospitals.

The ability of residents at private hospitals to organize and bargain represents an important breakthrough, and not only for the quality of life and political experience of the members themselves. These "professional workers-in-training" have traditionally been aligned with management. Aligned with organized labor, they offer other workers, both unionized and non-unionized, powerful allies in future fights.

One of those fights is to reduce the impact of market pressures on patient care. Just weeks before the union election, St. Luke's-Roosevelt announced plans to phase out its residency program in pediatrics. Competition from larger, more specialized facilities, management claimed, made pediatrics a less attractive investment. Administrators insist that the hospital's pediatric clinics, which serve parts of Harlem and midtown Manhattan, will stay open. But it is difficult to see how they will find high-quality physicians to staff the clinics – willing to do the work residents now perform – without exceeding current costs. Pediatrics is just one of the many casualties in affordability and access to quality health care, as hospitals prioritize "money makers" in struggling systems.

Already, residents, nurses, and other health care workers (like technicians and housekeepers) have taken common stands around issues such as work hours, unsafe needlestick exposure, and state and federal funding cuts – and have won. At St. Luke's-Roosevelt, members of 1199 (New York's health care workers' union) and CIR/SEIU are joining with community groups and local politicians, in hopes of preserving pediatric services and alleviating the staffing crisis that affects patient care and working conditions in all departments.

Stephanie Greenwood is a Dollars & Sense *intern.*

Article 30

SOCIAL MOVEMENTS ARE GOOD FOR YOUR HEALTH

BY THAD WILLIAMSON
May/June 2001

You come home from a long day at work, hungry and a little cranky. There's a couch inviting you to rest your weary head, and perhaps a promising ball game (or the next episode of *Survivor* on TV. No one could blame you if you just kicked back and called it a night. Why should you drag yourself out of the house again for that eight o'clock meeting to plan a local fair housing campaign, organize a statehouse protest, or even help edit articles for *Dollars & Sense?*

That's a question almost everybody who participates in social activism asks now and then. And the usual answer—and probably the best answer—is that the cause, the project, and magazine is worth the extra effort.

Bur for days when the payoff for that extra effort seems far off, and you're awfully comfortable on that couch, here's another answer: Going to meetings—being part of a social movement—is good for your health. You'll live longer, be happier, and feel better about yourself.

That's one of the striking findings of Robert Putnam's book, *Bowling Alone*, which analyzes the decline of social ties and community life in the United States. While some of Putnam's conclusions about the cause of that decline are controversial, almost no one disputes the proposition that social ties and strong communities are important to human well-being. And, as Putnam demonstrates, in no area is the link more clearly established than health.

According to Putnam, dozens of studies have shown that people who are more involved in community life have better physical and psychological health than the people who are socially isolated. Consider these basic facts:

In rich nations like the United States, Japan, and the Scandinavian countries, the annual death rate (holding age, gender, and other factors constant) for socially isolated people is at least twice as high as the death rate for people who have strong community ties. Joining an organization if you don't already belong to one has an impact on physical health roughly equivalent to quitting smoking.

Or if you're not ready to think about your own mortality, consider the case of the common cold. A 1997 study in the *Journal of American Medical Association* found that people with vibrant social networks are less likely to catch cold. Other studies have shown similar relationships between community involvement and recovery from stroke and depression.

Survey data compiled by the marketing firm DDB/Needham shows that active participation in community organizations greatly increases self-reported subjective well-being—the extend to which people are likely to say they are happy. In fact, a person inactive in community life would have to double her income to gain the same increase in happiness that she would derive from become an activist.

To be sure, the many studies and surveys cited by Putnam do not seem to indicate that one must join an organization that is political in nature to derive health benefits. And as anyone with much experience in activism knows, trying to make social change happen is often stressful, and too many commitments can cause a different kind of health problem: burnout. The health dividend from social activism consists mostly in the jump from going to no or few meetings to attending one or two a month—not in people who already go to five or six meetings a month finding time for two or three more.

But that fact simply reinforces the observation that making meaningful progressive social change happen in the United States in mainly a matter, not of getting the many thousands of people already intensely involved in activist efforts to do even more, but of finding ways to draw in the many millions who are doing relatively little. Take national health-care policy: If universal health coverage is ever to be achieved in the United States, it will require both favorable political circumstances and the mobilization of millions of Americans.

Such a social movement, if it achieved its policy goals, could improve health care delivery for millions of people. But what Putnam's work suggests is that the very creation of a social movement that brought fresh blood and new faces to meetings and rallies would have positive health effects, even before the first policy goal was met.

So the next time you feel tempted to stay home, go ahead and go to that movement meeting—and better yet, bring a friend along. Whether or not this week's cause turns out to be a winning fight, the very act of showing up increases the odds you'll be around to help win the next one—and the one after that.

Thad Williamson is a member of the Dollars & Sense *collective.*

Article 31

PRICE GOUGING: IT'S JUST SUPPLY AND DEMAND

MARC BRESLOW
September/October 2000

- May 2000: Growing demand, along with supply cutbacks by OPEC, lead to soaring gasoline prices around the United States, especially in the upper Midwest, where they reach $2 a gallon, almost twice the levels of a year earlier.
- September 2000: Both presidential candidates, George W. Bush and Al Gore, offer plans to prevent dramatic increases in the price of heating oil during the coming winter, due to expected supply shortages.
- 1999 and 2000: red-hot high-tech economies in the San Francisco Bay and Boston areas draw in more professional workers, and raise the demand for housing. Vacancy rates dwindle to near zero, and prices for both rentals and house purchases rise out of sight. Moderate- and low-income renters are evicted for non-payment and forced to move into smaller quarters or out of these metropolitan areas.

Critics of the oil industry charge that the companies are conspiring to raise prices during shortages, ripping off consumers and gaining huge profits through illegal behavior. The industries respond that there is no conspiracy, prices are rising due to the simple functioning of supply and demand in the market. The media debate the question: can evidence be found of a conspiracy? Or are rising prices simply due to increased costs as supplies are short? Politicians ask whether companies are guilty of illegal activity, and demand that investigations be opened.

What's going on? In reality, critics of the industries are missing the point of how a capitalist "free market" operates during times of shortages. The industry spokespersons are more on target in their explanations—but that doesn't mean what the companies are doing is okay. In fact, they *are* profiting at the expense of everyone who is forced to pay outrageous prices.

Both the media and public officials want to know whether rising costs of operation are causing the high prices, and therefore the companies are justified. Why? Because simple textbook economics says that in a competitive market we should get charged according to costs, with companies only making a "normal" profit. But a careful reading of the texts shows that this is only in the "long run" when new supplies can come into the market. In the short run, when a shortage develops, "supply and demand" can force prices up to unbelievable levels, especially for any product or service that is really a necessity. It doesn't have any relationship to the cost of supplying the item, nor does it take a conspiracy. The industry spokespeople are right that market pressures are the cause.

What confuses consumers is why a relatively small shortage can cause such a huge price jump, as it did for gasoline and electricity. Why, if OPEC reduces world oil supplies by only 1% or 2%, can the price of gasoline rise by perhaps 50%? Why shouldn't prices rise by the 1% or 2%? The answer lies in a common-sense understanding of what happens during a shortage. Everyone who owns a car, and still needs to get to work, drop the kids off at child care, and buy groceries, still needs to drive. In the short run, you can't sell your car for a more energy-efficient one, nor move someplace where public transit is more available, nor find a new day care center closer to home. Even if there are subways or buses available where you live, tight work and family time schedules probably make it difficult for you to leave the car at home.

So, as prices rise, everyone continues trying to buy as much gasoline as they did before (in technical terms, the "short run price elasticity of demand" is very low). But there is 2% less gas available, so not everyone can get as much as they want. Prices will continue rising until some people drop out of the market, cutting back on their purchases because they simply can't afford to pay the higher prices. For something as essential to modern life as gasoline, this can take quite a price jump. If the price goes from $1.20 to $1.30 will you buy less? How about $1.50? Or $1.80? You can see the problem. Prices can easily rise by 50% before demand falls by the 2% needed for supply and demand to equalize.

Note that this situation has nothing to do with the costs of supplying gasoline, nor do oil companies in the United States have to conspire together to raise prices. All they have to do is let consumers bid for the available gasoline. Nothing illegal has taken place—OPEC is acting as a cartel, "conspiring," but the United States has no legal power over other countries. Profits can go up enormously, and they may be shared between OPEC, oil companies such as Exxon/Mobil and Royal Dutch Shell, and firms lower on the supply chain such as wholesalers and retail gas stations.

Housing is perhaps the worst of these situations, as no one should be forced to leave their home. But the "invisible hand" of the market will raise prices, and allocate housing, according to who has the greatest purchasing power, not who needs the housing. A highly-skilled computer programmer, moving into San Francisco from elsewhere, will get an apartment that some lesser-paid worker, maybe a public school teacher or a bus driver, has been living in, perhaps for many years.

In all these cases, the market has done what it does well—allocate sales to those who can afford to buy, without regard to need; and allocate profits to those who have a product in short supply, without regard to costs of production. The human costs to people of moderate- and low-incomes, who are priced out of the market, can be severe. But they can be prevented—by price controls that prevent price-gouging due to shortages. Such controls have been used many times in the United States—for rent in high-demand cities, for oil and gas during the "crises" of the 1970's, and for most products during World War II. Maybe it's time we made them a staple of sensible economic policy.

Marc Breslow is co-chair of the Massachusetts Climate Action Network and a former member of the Dollars & Sense *collective.*

RESOURCES: "In Gas Prices, Misery and Mystery," Pam Belluck, *The New York Times*, 6/14/2000; "Federal action sought to cut power prices from May," Peter J. Howe, *The Boston Globe*, 8/24/2000; "Industry Blames Chemical Additives for High Gas Prices," Matthew L. Wald, *The New York Times*, 6/26/2000.

Article 32

THE GROWTH CONSENSUS UNRAVELS

JONATHAN ROWE
July/August 1999

Economics has been called the dismal science, but beneath its gray exterior is a system of belief worthy of Pollyanna.

Yes, economists manage to see a dark cloud in every silver lining. Downturn follows uptick, and inflation rears its ugly head. But there's a story within that story—a gauzy romance, a lyric ode to Stuff. It's built into the language. A thing produced is called a "good," for example, no questions asked. The word is more than just a term of art. It suggests the automatic benediction which economics bestows upon commodities of any kind.

By the same token, an activity for sale is called a "service." In conventional economics there are no "dis-services," no actions that might be better left undone. The bank that gouges you with ATM fees, the lawyer who runs up the bill—such things are "services" so long as someone pays. If a friend or neighbor fixes your plumbing for free, it's not a "service" and so it doesn't count.

The sum total of these products and activities is called the Gross Domestic Product, or GDP. If the GDP is greater this year than last, then the result is called "growth." There is no bad GDP and no bad growth; economics does not even have a word for such a thing. It does have a word for less growth. In such a case, economists say growth is "sluggish" and the economy is in "recession." No matter what is growing—more payments to doctors because of worsening health, more toxic cleanup—so long as there is more of it, then the economic mind declares it good.

This purports to be "objective science." In reality it is a rhetorical construct with the value judgments built in, and this rhetoric has been the basis of economic debate in the United States for the last half century at least. True, people have disagreed over how best to promote a rising GDP. Liberals generally wanted to use government more, conservatives less. But regarding the beneficence of a rising GDP, there has been little debate at all.

If anything, the Left traditionally has believed in growth with even greater fervor than the Right. It was John Maynard Keynes, after all, who devised the growth-boosting mechanisms of macroeconomic policy to combat the Depression of the 1930s; it was Keynesians who embraced these strategies after the war and turned the GDP into a totem. There's no point in seeking a bigger pie to redistribute to the poor, if you don't believe the expanding pie is desirable in the first place.

Today, however, the growth consensus is starting to unravel across the political spectrum and in ways that are both obvious and subtle. The issue is no longer just the impact of growth upon the environment—the toxic impacts of industry and the like. It now goes deeper, to what growth actually consists of and what it means in people's lives. The things economists call "goods" and "services" increasingly don't strike people as such. There is a growing disconnect between the way people experience growth and the way the policy establishment talks about it, and this gap is becoming an unspoken subtext to much of American political life.

The group most commonly associated with an antigrowth stance is environmentalists, of course. To be sure, one faction, the environmental economists, is trying to put green new wine into the old bottles of economic thought. If we would just make people pay the "true" cost of, say, the gasoline they burn, through the tax system for example, then the market would do the rest. We'd have benign, less-polluting growth, they say, perhaps even more than now. But the core of the environmental movement remains deeply suspicious of the growth ethos, and probably would be even if the environmental impacts somehow could be lessened.

In the middle are suburbanites who applaud growth in the abstract, but oppose the particular manifestations they see around them—the traffic, sprawl and crowded schools. On the Right, meanwhile, an anti-growth politics is arising practically unnoticed. When social conservatives denounce gambling, pornography, or sex and violence in the media, they are talking about specific instances of the growth that their political leaders rhapsodize on other days.

Environmentalists have been like social conservatives in one key respect. They have been moralistic regarding growth, often scolding people for enjoying themselves at the expense of future generations and the earth. Their concern is valid, up to a point—the consumer culture does promote the time horizon of a five year old. But politically it is not the most promising line of attack, and conceptually it concedes too much ground. To moralize about consumption as they do is to accept the conventional premise that it really is something chosen—an enjoyable form of self-indulgence that has unfortunate consequences for the earth.

That's "consumption" in the common parlance—the sport utility vehicle loading up at Wal-Mart, the stuff piling up in the basement and garage. But increasingly that's not what people actually experience, nor is it what the term really means. In economics, consumption means everything people spend money on, pleasurable or not. Wal-Mart is just one dimension of a much larger and increasingly unpleasant whole. The lawyers' fees for the house settlement or divorce; the repair work on the car after it was rear-ended; the cancer treatments for the uncle who was a three-pack-a-day smoker; the stress medications and weight loss regimens—all these and more are "consumption." They all go into the GDP.

Cancer treatments and lawyer's fees are not what come to mind when environmentalists lament the nation's excess consumption, or for that matter when economists applaud America's "consumers" for keeping the world economy afloat. Yet increasingly such things are what consumption actually consists of in the economy today. More and more, it consists not of pleasurable things that people choose, but rather of things that most people would gladly do without.

Much consumption today is addictive, for example. Millions of Americans are engaged in a grim daily struggle with themselves to do less of it. They want to eat less, drink less, smoke less, gamble less, talk less on the telephone—do less buying, period. Yet economic reasoning declares as growth and progress, that which people themselves regard as a tyrannical affliction.

Economists resist this reality of a divided self, because it would complicate their models beyond repair. They cling instead to an 18th century model of human psychology—the "rational" and self-interested man—which assumes those complexities away. As David McClelland, the Harvard psychologist, once put it, economists "haven't even discovered Freud, let alone Abraham Maslow." (They also haven't discovered the Apostle Paul, who lamented that "the good that I would I do not, but the evil that I would not that I do.")

Then too there's the mounting expenditure that sellers foist upon people through machination and deceit. People don't choose to pay for the corrupt campaign finance system or for bloated executive pay packages. The cost of these is hidden in the prices that we pay at the store. As I write this, the *Washington Post* is reporting that Microsoft has hired Ralph Reed, former head of the Christian Coalition, and Grover Norquist, a right-wing polemicist, as lobbyists in Washington. When I bought this computer with Windows 95, Bill Gates never asked me whether I wanted to help support a bunch of Beltway operators like these.

This is compulsory consumption, not choice, and the economy is rife with it today. People don't choose to pay some $40 billion a year in telemarketing fraud. They don't choose to pay 32% more for prescription drugs than do people in Canada. ("Free trade" means that corporations are free to buy their labor and materials in other countries, but ordinary Americans aren't equally free to do their shopping there.) For that matter, people don't choose to spend $25 and up for inkjet printer cartridges. The manufacturers design the printers to make money on the cartridges because, as the *Wall Street Journal* put it, that's "where the big profit margins are."

Yet another category of consumption that most people would gladly do without arises from the need to deal with the offshoots and implications of growth. Bottled water has become a multibillion dollar business in the United States because people don't trust what comes from the tap. There's a growing market for sound insulation and double-pane windows because the economy produces so much noise. A wide array of physical and social stresses arise from the activities that get lumped into the euphemistic term "growth."

The economy in such cases doesn't solve problems so much as create new problems that require more expenditure to solve. Food is supposed to sustain people, for example. But today the dis-economies of eating sustain the GDP instead. The food industry spends some $21 billion a year on advertising to entice people to eat food they don't need. Not coincidentally there's now a $32 billion diet and weight loss industry to help people take off the pounds that inevitably result. When that doesn't work, which is often, there is always the vacuum pump or knife. There were some 110,000 liposuctions in the United States last year; at five pounds each that's some 275 tons of flab up the tube.

It is a grueling cycle of indulgence and repentance, binge and purge. Yet each stage of this miserable experience, viewed through the pollyanic lens of economics, becomes growth and therefore good. The problem here goes far beyond the old critique of how the consumer culture cultivates feelings of inadequacy, lack and need so people will buy and buy again. Now this culture actually makes life worse, in order to sell solutions that purport to make it better.

Traffic shows this syndrome in a finely developed form. First we build sprawling suburbs so people need a car to go almost anywhere. The resulting long commutes are daily torture but help build up the GDP. Americans spend some $5 billion a year in gasoline alone while they sit in traffic and go nowhere. As the price of gas increases this growth sector will expand.

Commerce deplores a vacuum, and the exasperating hours in the car have spawned a booming subeconomy of relaxation tapes, cell phones, even special bibs. Billboards have 1-800 numbers so commuters can shop while they stew. Talk radio thrives on traffic-bound commuters, which accounts for some of the contentious, get-out-of-my-face tone. The traffic also helps sustain a $130 billion a year car wreck industry; and if Gates succeeds in getting computers into cars, that sector should get a major boost.

The health implications also are good for growth. Los Angeles, which has the worst traffic in the nation, also leads—if that's the word—in hospital admissions due to respiratory ailments. The resulting medical bills go into the GDP. And while Americans sit in traffic they aren't walking or getting exercise. More likely they are entertaining themselves orally with a glazed donut or a Big Mac, which helps explain why the portion of middle-aged Americans who are clinically obese has doubled since the 1960s.

C. Everett Koop, the former Surgeon General, estimates that some 70% of the nation's medical expenses are lifestyle induced. Yet the same lifestyle that promotes disease also produces a rising GDP. (Keynes observed that traditional virtues like thrift are bad for growth; now it appears that health is bad for growth too.) We literally are growing ourselves sick, and this puts a grim new twist on the economic doctrine of "complementary goods," which describes the way new products tend to spawn a host of others. The automobile gave rise to car wash franchises, drive-in restaurants, fuzz busters, tire dumps, and so forth. Television produced an antenna industry, VCRs, soap magazines, ad infinitum. The texts present this phenomenon as the wondrous perpetual motion machine of the market— goods beget more goods. But now the machine is producing complementary ills and collateral damages instead.

Suggestive of this new dynamic is a pesticide plant in Richmond, California, which is owned by a transnational corporation that also makes the breast cancer drug tamoxifen. Many researchers believe that pesticides, and the toxins created in the production of them, play a role in breast cancer. "It's a pretty good deal," a local physician told the East Bay Express, a Bay Area weekly. "First you cause the cancer, then you profit from curing it." Both the alleged cause and cure make the GDP go up, and this syndrome has become a central dynamic of growth in the U.S. today.

Mainstream economists would argue that this is all beside the point. If people didn't have to spend money on such things as commuting or medical costs, they'd simply spend it on something else, they say. Growth would be the same or even greater, so the actual content of growth should be of little concern to those who promote it. That view holds sway in the nation's policy councils; as a result we try continually to grow our way out of problems, when increasingly we are growing our way in.

To the extent conventional economics has raised an eyebrow at growth, it has done so mainly through the concept of "externalities." These are negative side effects suffered by those not party to a transaction between a buyer and a seller. Man buys car, car pollutes air, others suffer that "externality." As the language implies, anything outside the original transaction is deemed secondary, a subordinate reality, and therefore easily overlooked. More, the effects upon buyer and seller—the "internalities," one might say—are assumed to be good.

Today, however, that mental schema is collapsing. Externalities are starting to overwhelm internalities. A single jet ski can cause more misery for the people who reside by a lake, than it gives pleasure to the person riding it.

More importantly, and as just discussed, internalities themselves are coming into question, and with them the assumption of choice, which is the moral linchpin of market thought.

If people choose what they buy, as market theory posits, then—externalities aside—the sum total of all their buying must be the greatest good of all. That's the ideology behind the GDP. But if people don't always choose, then the model starts to fall apart, which is what is happening today. The practical implications are obvious. If growth consists increasingly of problems rather than solutions, then scolding people for consuming too much is barking up the wrong tree. It is possible to talk instead about ridding our lives of what we don't want as well as forsaking what we do want—or think we want.

Politically this is a more promising path. But to where? The economy may be turning into a kind of round robin of difficulty and affliction, but we are all tied to the game. The sickness industry employs a lot of people, as do ad agencies and trash haulers. The fastest-growing occupations in the country include debt collectors and prison guards. What would we do without our problems and dysfunctions?

The problem is especially acute for those at the bottom of the income scale who have not shared much in the apparent prosperity. For them, a bigger piece of a bad pie might be better than none.

This is the economic conundrum of our age. No one has more than pieces of an answer, but it helps to see that much growth today is really an optical illusion created by accounting tricks. The official tally ignores totally the cost side of the growth ledger—the toll of traffic upon our time and health for example. In fact, it actually counts such costs as growth and gain. By the same token, the official tally ignores the economic contributions of the natural environment and the social structure; so that the more the economy destroys these, and puts commoditized substitutes in their places, the more the experts say the economy has "grown." Pollute the lakes and oceans so that people have to join private swim clubs and the economy grows. Erode the social infrastructure of community so people have to buy services from the market instead of getting help from their neighbors, and it grows some more. The real economy—the one that sustains us—has diminished. All that has grown is the need to buy commoditized substitutes for things we used to have for free.

So one might rephrase the question thus: how do we achieve real growth, as opposed to the statistical illusion that passes for growth today? Four decades ago, John Kenneth Galbraith argued in The Affluent Society that conventional economic reasoning is rapidly becoming obsolete. An economics based upon scarcity simply doesn't work in an economy of hyper-abundance, he said. If it takes a $200 billion (today) advertising industry to maintain what economists quaintly call "demand," then perhaps that demand isn't as urgent as conventional theory posits. Perhaps it's not even demand in any sane meaning of the word.

Galbraith argued that genuine economy called for shifting some resources from consumption that needs to be prodded, to needs which are indisputably great: schools, parks, older people, the inner cities and the like. For this he was skewered as a proto-socialist. Yet today the case is even stronger, as advertisers worm into virtually every waking moment in a desperate effort to keep the growth machine on track.

Galbraith was arguing for a larger public sector. But that brings dysfunctions of its own, such as bureaucracy; and it depends upon an enlarging private sector as a fiscal base to begin with. Today we need to go further, and establish new ground rules for the economy, so that it produces more genuine growth on its own. We also need to find ways to revive the nonmarket economy of informal community exchange, so that people do not need money to meet every single life need.

In the first category, environmental fiscal policy can help. While the corporate world has flogged workers to be more productive, resources such as petroleum have been in effect loafing on the job. If we used these more efficiently the result could be jobs and growth, even in conventional terms, with less environmental pollution. If we used land more efficiently—that is, reduced urban sprawl—the social and environmental gains would be great.

Another ground rule is the corporate charter laws. We need to restore these to their original purpose: to keep large business organizations within the compass of the common good. But such shifts can do only so much. More efficient cars might simply encourage more traffic, for example. Cheap renewable power for electronic devices could encourage more noise. In other words, the answer won't just be a more efficient version of what we do now. Sooner or later we'll need different ways of thinking about work and growth and how we allocate the means of life.

This is where the social economy comes in, the informal exchange between neighbors and friends. There are some promising trends. One is the return to the traditional village model in housing. Structure does affect content. When houses are close together, and people can walk to stores and work, it encourages the spontaneous social interaction that nurtures real community. New local currencies, such as Time Dollars, provide a kind of lattice work upon which informal nonmarket exchange can take root and grow.

Changes like these are off the grid of economics as conventionally defined. It took centuries for the market to emerge from the stagnation of feudalism. The next organizing principle, whatever it is, most likely will emerge slowly as well. This much we can say with certainty. As the market hurtles towards multiple implosions, social and environmental as well as financial, it is just possible that the economics profession is going to have to do what it constantly lectures the rest of us to do: adjust to new realities and show a willingness to change.

Jonathan Rowe is a contributing editor at the Washington Monthly.

Article 33

THE "NATURAL RATE" OF UNEMPLOYMENT
It's all about class conflict.

ROBERT POLLIN
September/October 1997

In 1997, the official U.S. unemployment rate fell to a 27-year low of 4.9%. Most orthodox economists had long predicted that a rate this low would lead to uncontrollable inflation. So they argued that maintaining a higher unemployment rate—perhaps as high as 6%—was crucial for keeping the economy stable. But there is a hitch: last year the inflation rate was 2.3%, the lowest figure in a decade and the second lowest in 32 years. What then are we to make of these economists' theories, much less their policy proposals?

Nobel Prize-winning economist Milton Friedman gets credit for originating the argument that low rates of unemployment would lead to accelerating inflation. His 1968 theory of the so-called "natural rate of unemployment" was subsequently developed by many mainstream economists under the term "Non-Accelerating Inflation Rate of Unemployment," or NAIRU, a remarkably clumsy term for expressing the simple concept of a threshold unemployment rate below which inflation begins to rise.

According to both Friedman and expositors of NAIRU, inflation should accelerate at low rates of unemployment because low unemployment gives workers excessive bargaining power. This allows the workers to demand higher wages. Capitalists then try to pass along these increased wage costs by raising prices on the products they sell. An inflationary spiral thus ensues as long as unemployment remains below its "natural rate."

Based on this theory, Friedman and others have long argued that governments should never actively intervene in the economy to promote full employment or better jobs for workers, since it will be a futile exercise, whose end result will only be higher inflation and no improvement in job opportunities. Over the past generation, this conclusion has had far-reaching influence throughout the world. In the United States and Western Europe, it has provided a stamp of scientific respectability to a whole range of policies through which governments abandoned even modest commitments to full employment and workers' rights.

This emerged most sharply through the Reaganite and Thatcherite programs in the United States and United Kingdom in the 1980s. But even into the 1990s, as the Democrats took power in the United States, the Labour Party won office in Britain, and Social Democrats won elections throughout Europe, governments remained committed to stringent fiscal and monetary policies, whose primary goal is to prevent inflation. In Western Europe this produced an average unemployment rate of over 10% from 1990-97. In the United States, unemployment rates have fallen sharply in the 1990s, but as an alternative symptom of stringent fiscal and monetary policies, real wages for U.S. workers also declined dramatically over the past generation. As of 1997, the average real wage for non-supervisory workers in the United States was 14% below its peak in 1973, even though average worker productivity rose between 1973 and 1997 by 34%.

Why have governments in the United States and Europe remained committed to the idea of fiscal and monetary stringency, if the natural rate theory on which such policies are based is so obviously flawed? The explanation is that the natural rate theory is really not just about predicting a precise unemployment rate figure below which inflation must inexorably accelerate, even though many mainstream economists have presented the natural rate theory in this way. At a deeper level, the natural rate theory is bound up with the inherent conflicts between workers and capitalists over jobs, wages, and working conditions. As such, the natural rate theory actually contains a legitimate foundation in truth amid a welter of sloppy and even silly predictions.

The "Natural Rate" Theory Is About Class Conflict

In his 1967 American Economic Association presidential address in which he introduced the natural rate theory, Milton Friedman made clear that there was really nothing "natural" about the theory. Friedman rather emphasized that: "by using the term 'natural' rate of unemployment, I do not mean to suggest that it is immutable and unchangeable. On the contrary, many of the market characteristics that determine its level are man-made and policy-made. In the United States, for example, legal minimum wage rates…and the strength of labor unions all make the natural rate of unemployment higher than it would otherwise be."

In other words, according to Friedman, what he terms the "natural rate" is really a social phenomenon measuring the class strength of working people, as indicated by their ability to organize effective unions and establish a livable minimum wage.

Friedman's perspective is supported in a widely-read 1997 paper by Robert Gordon of Northwestern University on what he terms the "time-varying NAIRU." What makes the NAIRU vary over time? Gordon explains that, since the early 1960s, "The two especially large changes in the NAIRU… are the increase between the early and late 1960s and the decrease in the 1990s. The late 1960s were a time of labor militancy, relatively strong unions, a relatively high minimum wage and a marked increase in labor's share in national income. The 1990s have been a time of labor peace, relatively weak unions, a relatively low minimum wage and a slight decline in labor's income share."

In short, class conflict is the spectre haunting the analysis of the natural rate and NAIRU: this is the consistent message stretching from Milton Friedman in the 1960s to Robert Gordon in the 1990s.

Stated in this way, the "Natural Rate" idea does, ironically, bear a close family resemblance to the ideas of two of the greatest economic thinkers of the left, Karl Marx and Michal Kalecki, on a parallel concept—the so-called "Reserve Army of Unemployed." In his justly famous Chapter 25 of Volume I of *Capital*, "The General Law of Capitalist Accumulation," Marx argued forcefully that unemployment serves an important function in capitalist economies. That is, when a capitalist economy is growing rapidly enough so that the reserve army of unemployed is depleted, workers will then utilize their increased bargaining power to raise wages. Profits are correspondingly squeezed as workers get a larger share of the country's total income. As a result, capitalists anticipate further declines in profitability and they therefore reduce their investment spending. This then leads to a fall in job creation, higher unemployment, and a replenishment of the reserve army. In other words, the reserve army of the unemployed is the instrument capitalists use to prevent significant wage increases and thereby maintain profitability.

Kalecki, a Polish economist of the Great Depression era, makes parallel though distinct arguments in his also justly famous essay, "The Political Aspects of Full Employment." Kalecki wrote in 1943, shortly after the 1930s Depression had ended and governments had begun planning a postwar world in which they would deploy aggressive policies to avoid another calamity of mass unemployment. Kalecki held, contrary to Marx, that full employment can be beneficial to the profitability of businesses. True, capitalists may get a smaller share of the total economic pie as workers gain bargaining power to win higher wages. But capitalists can still benefit because the size of the pie is growing far more rapidly, since more goods and services can be produced when everyone is working, as opposed to some significant share of workers being left idle.

But capitalists still won't support full employment, in Kalecki's view, because it will threaten their control over the workplace, the pace and direction of economic activity, and even political institutions. Kalecki thus concluded that full employment could be sustainable under capitalism, but only if these challenges to capitalists' social and political power could be contained. This is why he held that fascist social and political institutions, such as those that existed in Nazi Germany when he was writing, could well provide one "solution" to capitalism's unemployment problem, precisely because they were so brutal. Workers would have jobs, but they would never be permitted to exercise the political and economic power that would otherwise accrue to them in a full-employment economy.

Broadly speaking, Marx and Kalecki do then share a common conclusion with natural rate proponents, in that they would all agree that positive unemployment rates are the outgrowth of class conflict over the distribution of income and political power. Of course, Friedman and other mainstream economists reach this conclusion via analytic and political perspectives that are diametrically opposite to those of Marx and Kalecki. To put it in a nutshell, in the Friedmanite view mass unemployment results when workers demand more than they deserve, while for Marx and Kalecki, capitalists use the weapon of unemployment to prevent workers from getting their just due.

From Natural Rate to Egalitarian Policy

Once the analysis of unemployment in capitalist economies is properly understood within the framework of class conflict, several important issues in our contemporary economic situation become much more clear. Let me raise just a few:

1. Mainstream economists have long studied how workers' wage demands cause inflation as unemployment falls. However, such wage demands never directly cause inflation, since inflation refers to a general rise in prices of goods and services sold

in the market, not a rise in wages. Workers, by definition, do not have the power to raise prices. Capitalists raise prices on the products they sell. At low unemployment, inflation occurs when capitalists respond to workers' increasingly successful wage demands by raising prices so that they can maintain profitability. If workers were simply to receive a higher share of national income, then lower unemployment and higher wages need not cause inflation at all.

2. There is little mystery as to why, at present, the so-called "time-varying" NAIRU has diminished to a near vanishing point, with unemployment at a 25-year low while inflation remains dormant. The main explanation is the one stated by Robert Gordon—that workers' economic power has been eroding dramatically through the 1990s. Workers have been almost completely unable to win wage increases over the course of the economic expansion that by now is seven years old.

3. This experience over the past seven years, with unemployment falling but workers showing almost no income gains, demonstrates dramatically the crucial point that full employment can never stand alone as an adequate measure of workers' well-being. This was conveyed vividly to me when I was working in Bolivia in 1990 as part of an economic advising team led by Keith Griffin of the University of California-Riverside. Professor Griffin asked me to examine employment policies.

I began by paying a visit to the economists at the Ministry of Planning. When I requested that we discuss the country's employment problems, they explained, to my surprise, that the country had no employment problems. When I suggested we consider the situation of the people begging, shining shoes, or hawking batteries and Chiclets in the street just below the window where we stood, their response was that these people were employed. And of course they were, in that they were actively trying to scratch out a living. It was clear that I had to specify the problem at hand far more precisely. Similarly, in the United States today, we have to be much more specific as to what workers should be getting in a fair economy: jobs, of course, but also living wages, benefits, reasonable job security, and a healthy work environment.

4. In our current low-unemployment economy, should workers, at long last, succeed in winning higher wages and better benefits, some inflationary pressures are likely to emerge. But if inflation does not accelerate after wage increases are won, this would mean that businesses are not able to pass along their higher wage costs to their customers. Profits would therefore be squeezed. In any case, in response to either inflationary pressures or a squeeze in profitability, we should expect that many, if not most, segments of the business community will welcome a Federal Reserve policy that would slow the economy and raise the unemployment rate.

Does this mean that, as long as we live in a capitalist society, the control by capitalists over the reserve army of labor must remain the dominant force establishing the limits of workers' strivings for jobs, security, and living wages? The challenge for the progressive movement in the United States today is to think through a set of policy ideas through which full employment at living wages can be achieved and sustained.

Especially given the dismal trajectory of real wage decline over the past generation, workers should of course continue to push for wage increases. But it will also be crucial to advance these demands within a broader framework of proposals. One important component of a broader package would be policies through which labor and capital bargain openly over growth of wages and profits after full employment is achieved. Without such an open bargaining environment, workers, with reason, will push for higher wages once full employment is achieved, but capitalists will then respond by either raising prices or favoring high unemployment. Such open bargaining policies were conducted with considerable success in Sweden and other Nordic countries from the 1950s to the 1980s, and as a result, wages there continued to rise at full employment, while both accelerating inflation and a return to high unemployment were prevented.

Such policies obviously represent a form of class compromise. This is intrinsically neither good nor bad. The question is the terms under which the compromise is achieved. Wages have fallen dramatically over the past generation, so workers deserve substantial raises as a matter of simple fairness. But workers should also be willing to link their wage increases to improvements in productivity growth, i.e., the rate at which workers produce new goods and services. After all, if the average wage had just risen at exactly the rate of productivity growth since 1973 and not a penny more, the average hourly wage today for non-supervisory workers would be $19.07 rather than $12.24.

But linking wages to improvements in productivity then also raises the question of who controls the decisions that determine the rate of productivity growth. In fact, substantial productivity gains are attainable through operating a less hierarchical workplace and building strong democratic unions through which workers can defend their rights on the job. Less hierarchy and increased workplace democracy creates higher morale on the job, which in turn increases workers' effort and opportunities to be inventive, while decreasing turnover and absenteeism. The late David Gordon of the New School for Social Research was among the leading analysts demonstrating how economies could operate more productively through greater workplace democracy.

But improvements in productivity also result from both the public and private sector investing in new and better machines that workers put to use every day, with the additional benefit that it means more jobs for people who produce those machines. A pro-worker economic policy will therefore also have to be concerned with increasing investments to improve the stock of machines that workers have at their disposal on the job.

In proposing such a policy approach, have I forgotten the lesson that Marx and Kalecki taught us, that unemployment serves a purpose in capitalism? Given that this lesson has become part of the standard mode of thinking among mainstream economists ranging from Milton Friedman to Robert Gordon, I would hope that I haven't let it slip from view. My point nevertheless is that through changing power relationships at the workplace and the decision-making process through which investment decisions get made, labor and the left can then also achieve a more egalitarian economy, one in which capitalists' power to brandish the weapon of unemployment is greatly circumscribed. If the labor movement and the left neglect issues of control over investment and the workplace, we will continue to live amid a Bolivian solution to the unemployment problem, where full employment is the by-product of workers' vulnerability, not their strength.

Robert Pollin teaches economics and is co-director of the Political Economy Research Institute at the University of Massachusetts at Amherst. He is also a Dollars & Sense *Associate.*

RESOURCES: A longer version of this article appears as "The 'Reserve Army of Labor' and the 'Natural Rate of Unemployment': Can Marx, Kalecki, Friedman, and Wall Street All Be Wrong?," *Review of Radical Political Economics*, Fall 1998. Both articles derive from a paper originally presented as the David Gordon Memorial Lecture at the 1997 Summer Conference of the Union for Radical Political Economics. See also Robert Pollin and Stephanie Luce, *The Living Wage: Building A Fair Economy*, 1998; David Gordon, *Fat and Mean*, 1997; David Gordon, "Generating Affluence: Productivity Gains Require Worker Support," *Real World Macro*, 15th ed., 1998.

Printed in the United States
123600LV00002B/316-474/P